Author shows how evolving comes i
mistakes which are not really mistake.   ...ing
our talk and sometimes tripping up a fe   ...erore we
finally get the message about what we need in order to grow
NEW DAWN MAGAZINE

Absorb yourself within these pages. The author is a body
language psychologist and runs workshops helping people to
live a more auspicious life
PSYCHIC NEWS MAGAZINE

Dean Fraser sees his mission in life to spread some much-
needed laughter and love in this world
INDIE SHAMAN MAGAZINE

The sooner more know about The Two Minute De-Stress, the
sooner we can bring more peace to the world
MORE TO LIFE MAGAZINE

Thought provokingly deep
LANCASHIRE LIVING MAGAZINE

Dean was very interactive with the audience afterwards and
from that, he has offered to come back to do a session on how
to meditate – a request from the audience
CHESTER & CHESHIRE WEST COUNCIL

343 pages of poems by Dean Fraser

We all deserve to be happier, healthier and more successful, let me show you why and how!

Dedicated to all of us seekers of more than a treadmill existence – those looking to have a fuller, happier experience on this amazing planet of ours.

In this life we live by our own free will choice
Be quiet to listen to our own inner voice

ALIVE TO THRIVE

How to be Happier, Healthier
and More Successful

Dean Fraser

First published Worldwide in 2015 as YOU But Happier, Healthier and More Successful.

This updated edition 2019 Copyright © Dean Fraser.

Published by Alive To Thrive Ltd.

Dean Fraser has asserted his right under the Copyright, Designs and Patents Act 1988 to be identified as the author of this book and work.

ISBN 9781723954238

All quotes appearing in this book to begin each chapter are from the author, unless stated otherwise.

CONTENTS

www.deanfrasercentral.com

NOW IS THE TIME

The most wonderful way to experience all the magic
The magnificence that is called life
Is to live in the now
For the moment...it is the only reality

FOREWORD TO THE NEW EDITION

> **We all deserve to be happier, healthier and more successful, let me show you why and how!**

It's how we value ourselves, our personal idea of how much our knowledge and uniqueness are worth that determines the results we get from life.

I left school at 16 with a vague idea I wanted to work in publishing, no real plan, just that publishing kind of interested me. The first company I joined happened to be the largest in town, working for them quickly failed to ingnite much passion in me at all. My role seemed to be making tea and stacking shelves in the storeroom. I was learning nothing there. Yes, for sure I was still a kid, but I felt I was worth more than the value this company placed on my skills.

I lasted out a few weeks and moved on to a far smaller publishing house. Here I was thrown right in at the deep end straight away to see if I would swim. Pitching to potential clients on the phone within an hour of arriving on my first day. Now this might not be the conventional route of training a wet-behind-the-ears 16 year old in business. It worked though. Although I was still earning the same minimum wage, I felt valued.

I loved this job, once I overcame the nerves holding me back in those first few weeks, I thrived. Even with my lack of experience, because I felt appreciated and valued, I started to look around for possibilities where I might add value to the job, the company.

Of course, my big opportunity came when the manager of the contracts department I worked in left to pursue his own dream to be a lawyer. I found myself really swimming in the deep end when at 18 years old I got a three month probationary period to see if I could run the department. Well, okay the department had only consisted of the two of us, so in a sense I was now my own manager, anyway I was impressively titled the Acting Manager of Contracts, I even had the business card to prove it!

Long story short, I brought a million pounds worth of business into the company before my 20th birthday, while still a teenager. Doubling the turn-over of the company in the process.

With no real experience to fall back on I had nothing to lose so I just went out and had some fun, stretching myself and yes for sure adding a lot of value to the company, but way more importantly I proved to myself what I am truly capable of!

We are all capable of way more than we ever imagined possible and all that untapped potential is waiting right there within us ready to be released…

Did everything go smoothly? Was every day perfect? Of course not. For sure I had my learning opportunities along the way, some might label them mistakes, they only become a mistake if we keep on repeating them and don't learn to do things differently next time.

I found myself at 18 years old earning more than five times my wages of just two year earlier. How? I didn't work harder or more hours than before; I was payed for results so I focused all of my attention on the major ways to get spectacular results! Here I was this teenager earning more than everyone else in the company apart from the managing director. Why? I knew I could and then went ahead to prove it!

It is how we value ourselves, our self-worth that matters the most. With the right mindset we can easily become happier or richer, and preferably both…

1

INTRODUCTION

The question, is our destiny truly our own to decide?
Does to follow other than destiny cause planets to collide?

The two year old boy had an issue with his feet and legs. Somehow, they had failed to so far develop exactly as they needed to and his parents with due concern took him off to get checked-out firstly by their GP and then after referral, to a specialist. His legs were not growing quite as straight as they might, and a potential future of limited physical ability was all too real a possibility. Operating remained an option, however, rather than going for that more intrusive approach at this stage, instead it was suggested that intensive physiotherapy might strengthen his muscles and get everything back on track.

Although still under three years old, the situation was accessibly explained to the boy and the reality that doing

15

his daily exercises, combined with much walking would give him a great chance of his legs and feet becoming naturally corrected to grow properly. With sheer force of will he did precisely that (his mum also got extremely fit in the process!) as the young boy firmly insisted on walking absolutely anywhere and everywhere it was at all possible to. And it worked, developing the muscle mass in his legs eventually brought everything back to where it needed to be. Just prior to reaching his teens, the boy's feet and legs had begun to grow much straighter and would continue to heal entirely.

He wasn't to know it at such a young age, but the boy was developing a cast-in-steel level of self-discipline. One which he was later able to apply after the climbing accident he experienced ten years later, injuring his lower back, left him once again with little choice but to work through the pain for six months to regain full mobility and fitness. By quietly walking dozens of miles each week, he eventually found the discomfort subsided, to leave him with an even more solidly inbuilt self-discipline and determination to succeed no matter what.

If there was one mindset I might be able to indelibly impress into the subconscious of every one of you who reads this book, it is this — **self-discipline and sheer determination will absolutely ensure you succeed, whatever!**

Power and being empowered has precious little to do with the traditional image of the aggressive warrior winning out against the world. It is our own quiet inner strength which wins-out every single time. No fuss, just getting on and doing it!

It did with me, the boy in the story and it will with you.

CHANGE BEGINS WITH YOU

Anyone and I don't care who they are, can change things to make their life more empowered and live a more successful lifestyle. By success I don't just mean having a big bank balance, it is about being rich in all the different areas of our lives. What is the point in being materially wealthy if all we are is ill or miserable all the time?

You or I are also going to want to know how to stay happy and healthy, to actively enjoy all the personal successes of our own it is possible for us to achieve.

There is an art to being empowered and although we certainly need to be passionate about our goals, we equally need to become a little detached from the way in which it all literally happens. This is one of the more challenging lessons for many of us to learn, including myself for a while, and remaining passionate yet detached is something which I will cover in more detail throughout the book.

The greatest martial artists in any discipline practise controlled power – here is true empowerment. The martial arts practitioner who uses only pure aggression or worse still anger, is unlikely to stay the course. And it is precisely the same for us when we walk the path of our goals.

The methods I describe in this book represent truly cutting-edge life changing techniques, having been quite naturally using them myself right from the beginning of my career (although at that point I wasn't necessarily aware of this!).

Gradually I became conscious that not everyone buys into or uses this mindset, and this became the defining moment for me, the point when I realised my mission needed to become showing others how to overcome any self-imposed limitation. Guiding them to also living a life of happiness and fulfilment.

The truth that this is genuinely possible for anyone (and not just a lucky few) to make the choice as a conscious decision to live their life this way. Never has the phrase **life is all about the attitude** been more relevant!

These tried and tested methods include:

- Learning to trust your intuition.
- Investing your actions with one ocean load of passion to discover your own personal life-plan.
- Working on a success orientated mindset.
- Staying focussed in the moment to ensure maximum effectiveness.
- Controlling of your own financial future by setting targets and finding ways to take direct action every day, however small, to achieve them.
- Also, how a few simple adjustments in lifestyle can dramatically reduce stress and equally importantly the likelihood of developing serious health issues.

Not everything is going to go perfectly as we anticipated every single day, the trick here is to keep on going anyway and not get distracted or start feeling sorry for yourself. The best way to improve our reality is to take personal responsibility for our own life and then get out there to make those changes we want for ourselves!

WHAT IS THE FIRST STEP TO THIS AMAZING NEW LIFE?

Deciding what it is we genuinely want!

Okay, you are probably wondering what the heck I am talking about, yes?

Surely all of us want to be successful, don't we?

 Well…that all depends.

You would be amazed how unresolved emotional baggage from the past can block you or I from achieving all we have the latent potential to.

If someone grew up in a home where parents always struggled with cash and as a child, they witnessed their friends getting cool presents for birthdays and they didn't; whichever way you look at it this person is going to have a few issues relating to money to overcome on their own personal road to success.

If you have got a bad track record with making and keeping money what were your experiences growing up? What did your parents say when you wanted something in a shop that you couldn't have? If it was more like "we can't afford that" or "there isn't enough money to buy you things all the time" it might well have set up feelings of anxiety about money. There will be never enough for everything, creating a kind of poor mentality self-fulfilling prophecy.

Parents naturally never mean to do this, they are just striving to making ends meet and once you are living big you can help them financially anyway if you choose, plus your own life is also going to be an example to all of your family and friends of what it is possible to achieve. More of which as we continue our journey through Alive to Thrive

For the moment though, let's get back to this **what do you really want?** question.

It is all down to what success means to you. To some this is going to be limitless amounts of cash, to others the freedom to do what they want without having to think about budgeting for it.

Many have the personal concept of success as helping others realise their own potential, while being healthily stress-free and all that combined together with possessing the financial freedom to able to afford to do more or less anything they wish.

Take some time to do this, ponder deeply about what you really want and that is half the trick complete…more about this later.

I am grateful for my own experiences as a young boy, they have helped me countless times in adulthood. The self-discipline required to keep on keeping on without buying-into distraction or displacements can be traced directly back to those earlier days.

And yet, determination and self-discipline can be anyone's at any time in our lives - all it requires is making the decision to empower ourselves.

2

THE TRUTH ABOUT THE ENERGY OF MONEY

It will happen. Life will change. The choice is yours. How much do you want it and how brave do you feel? Are you ready?

Money of itself is never the route to happiness. Any of us can achieve financial freedom if we remain single-minded enough. It is not going to mean an awful lot though if we are as miserable as the meanest miser is it? Money is there to be used and circulated around to attract more money.

By the way, living a rich lifestyle has precious little to do with just your bank balance. Enraptured by a beautiful sunset or waking early enough to witness sunrise, that is living rich…watching our children grow into fulfilled adults is richness beyond any amount of hard cash.

A QUESTION I GET ASKED MORE THAN ANY OTHER...

Q. Anyone at all can have financial freedom?

Me. Yes

Q. Is that genuinely true?

Me. It sure is, but happiness means so much more!

Back to money, for now...

It is all about the attitude of our habitual mindset relating to money. That maybe it is in some way impossible to be rich and have vast amounts of any kind of currency you can think of. I am here to say this is simply untrue and I am also willing to bet that you get this for yourself as you read on, that attitude is ALL when it comes to making it big financially.

Oh, and to be clear, I am not talking here about the one in a billion chance of winning the lottery! Far better to invest your weekly lottery stake in something to genuinely make you guaranteed money.

Instead I am talking about taking control yourself, of your own life by adopting a new mindset. Developing the ability to focus on what we truly want is vital. It would be all too easy to proclaim the easiest way to keep money is by not spending any, but obviously we have all got our commitments and needs to be met.

What we think about ourselves and our potential quite literally creates who we are and the experiences we have through life.

If I would love to be a scratch golfer, wishing alone doesn't automatically make me go around the course in par. I can make it work though if I mirror the mindset of a professional golfer I admire, together with perfectly copying the playing techniques to make it real, do this and the chances are soon I will be that scratch golfer!

What we programme our subconscious through our thoughts and words helps us to become our own idea of how we should look and be. And everyone does this constantly, regardless of if they are even aware of this.

Yet we have a choice. Our mindset is 100% in our own hands. As you read this book you are going to find some unique ways to eradicate anything from within your mindset which might possibly hold you back, buy-into the ones that speak to you...nobody can do this for us, it's all down to you and how much you want the freedom to finally live each day on your terms.

Our subconscious minds are constantly being programmed with our own conscious thoughts. And more alarmingly the thoughts of those around us if we care to listen to their opinions about who we are or what we ought to do in our life. It is all too easy to lose track of our own motivations, and even beliefs, if we pay too much attention to the constant stream of words coming our way from even well-meaning family and friends, never mind about those toxic people we all encounter from time to time!

DO YOU EVER THINK OF YOURSELF AS BEING POOR?

To be candidly blunt, if you do, you are going to be poor. Poor is a state of mind which does not serve anyone in any way! If you are low on funds right now realise that is a temporary situation. And it is a situation that can quickly change for the better by focussing attention on precisely how we can quickly change it for the better!

If you and I don't want to go through life being poor, we had better quickly re-programme our subconscious with more useful mindsets. There is always a way to turn-around temporary low funds through action, however leftfield that action might be. Now is the ideal time to put into practise some of the methods right here in this book to overcome any self-limiting thoughts to utilize your talents. Avoid labelling yourself poor! Jettison that poor mindset forever!!!

DARE TO THINK BIG!

I have had audience members and my clients state they would definitely like to have more money, but please not too much! Perhaps a few hundred thousand will be enough, but certainly not millions. That would apparently be way too stressful!

All they want to do is pay off their mortgage, cover their children's University fees, get a new car and maybe catch a few good vacations. These guys are limiting themselves completely and totally. Setting low targets about what they want to achieve. And yet they might do so much more…

Becoming financially successful can open so many doors. It is also inevitably though going to lead to a complete lifestyle change.

We do have to be prepared for the fact that having greater wealth does bring more responsibility, for sure.

Radical change in our lives can also lead to some personal acquaintances no longer being compatible within this new reality of ours. Personally, I found some old friendships do organically drift away. And talking to others in a similar reality confirms this is how it often plays out when we reach a new plateau of achievement. As our own Comfort Zone expands, some of those around us will not necessarily be able to adapt to this new reality and we need to be prepared for the fact that certain friendships (and actually sometimes even closer relationships) will no longer work.

You are going to need to employ a good accountant to reduce your taxable funds (donating some of your profits to a charity which is close to your heart is a great win/win) and further you will need to decide what you are going to do with your success; invest in property, businesses, buy shares or whatever else.

The tricks to growing your wealth are learned on the job as you go along, the advice of strategic accountants and PA's can always be listened to, but it is your gut instinct you have absolutely got to trust and go with in the end. We will return to this later…for now…

ASSETS AND LIABILITIES

Here is a fascinating question I usually ask which will generally provoke a passionate response from my audiences at my seminars **"What do you consider are the main <u>material</u> assets and liabilities in your life?"**

- Their answers on assets vary from cars, computers, houses, businesses, precious jewellery or any one of the other countless material items many of us value.
- Typically, their liabilities turn out to be bank or credit card loans to pay off, heavy mortgages or sometimes even their job!

Understandably there are many variations in fine detail within the answers my audiences offer as feedback, averagely though they do tend to narrow down to something along these similar themes.

Okay, time to again be a little candidly honest once more and risk courting controversy with these next statements, do keep an open mind and I promise you will see where I am coming from here:

1. Anything at all you are purchasing on any kind of a loan, which will end up being worth <u>less</u> than

you paid for it once the loan is complete and paid-up – this is a liability.

2. Anything at all which **adds material value to your life** or somehow **brings you closer your ideal reality**, in any way, however indirectly or abstractly - **this is an asset.**

Stress is all too often directly caused by living beyond our means, paying too much for those things which bring us absolutely no closer to our goals and in fact end up worth far less materially than we slogged away to purchase them for.

BEEN THERE, DONE THAT, LEARNED THE LESSON

When I first started to make a small profit for myself with my own first business (when I was done with working for others) I went out and bought myself a beautiful silver Jaguar car on credit.

Quite effectively tying-up a few hundred of my working capital every single month to meet those re-payments, money which might instead have been used to help grow my business by expanding my marketplace through buying advertising.

Quickly I came to look upon this car as entirely pointless, it sat right there in the car-park (depreciating more in value every week!) while I worked to pay for it. It added precisely nothing to my dreams, success mindset or for sure any sense of wellbeing. On the contrary I saw it as a large physical manifestation of a lesson learned and as soon as it was eventually payed for in full I promptly sold it the same day!

The station wagon I bought to replace it (at half the price of the Jaguar and this time not on credit) proved far more useful in the long run.

Since that learning experience I avoided buying anything on credit which does not either appreciate dramatically in value over an extremely short length of time or equally dramatically help me to realise goals.

Although it is unlikely I would (as I believe we need to follow our passion and whichever way I look at it, this fails to excite me) yet if I ever did decide to take out a mortgage it would be to buy houses to let out for tenants. Assets providing value, the mortgage effectively covered by the rent whilst I enjoy an annual yield in terms of profit.

OVER TO YOU

Ponder your own life, how many assets do you possess compared to liabilities?

At this point I know it won't be possible to change some things which you might now view as liabilities, rather than assets. Positively instead use this new-found perspective to inspire a long-term plan to turn around your life balance to possessing more assets than liabilities!

In the meantime, when we are making future financial commitments of any kind, honesty with ourselves pays long term dividends:

1. Will this commitment be a sound financial investment, in other words **add value materially or in terms of helping to attain your goals** in the fullness of time?
2. If the answer is yes, great you are looking at an asset!
3. If the answer is no, then you might want to seriously consider if this is something you really wish to buy-into or go ahead with.

Of course, once you have got unlimited funds available, absolutely indulge a little and treat yourself and your family to some of the non-profit making luxuries they can enjoy!

We love to travel visiting inspiring places, having the freedom to visit art galleries of our choice around the world or experience places of natural beauty is food for our souls indeed. Money is made to be circulated around and enjoyed. And studying success will ensure this wonderful freedom happens without further delay…

3

STUDENT OF SUCCESS

It being absolutely essential
To live our life to our potential.

We have a crucial need to develop trust in our intuition and grow the inner confidence to carve our own individual path…increase our value to the world.

Naturally then it is extremely useful to reinforce this by getting to know what makes other self-made successful people tick. Getting inside their heads to discover what it is they do that is so radically different from everyone else. Those who have been there and done that…especially within whatever area is our personal passion. Their mindset is invaluable to us.

Best way to do this is devour autobiographies, study interviews/vids online or in magazines and even those TV shows where members of the public pitch to business entrepreneurs. Learn what inspires and motivates these walking success stories. Find out why they get out of bed each morning and what they focus their energies on all day.

The kinds of energy we surround ourselves with is ALL IMPORTANT!

Take the opportunity to study the mindset of those already walking their talk within your area of interest; to obviously still be you, but consistently mirroring what you need within your actual daily focus to turbo-charge your dreams and making them far more likely to happen sooner rather than later!

You can choose to mirror the mindset of those high-achievers in whatever area interest you. This is never about giving-up on being you…it's about empowering yourself by utilizing other people's experience, especially useful if you have yet to have any experience of your own.

And you know what? 99.9% of all high-achievers will have done precisely the same as you are when they started out…including me!

Over the years I have devoured the information from more motivational, positive psychology and business books than I can count, watched thousands of hours of inspirational vids, firstly the old-fashioned way and then later online; and I still take care to do this each day. This self-empowering choice is how I ended up stood in front of thousands of people to help them on their path to whatever their own concept of living an amazing life might be.

Do your groundwork and you are way ahead of all those who passively wait around for their lives to change.

All the high-achievers within whatever area of their activity all share one thing in common; they are prepared to take a risk. They step outside of their comfort zone to do something new. But you can be darned sure they don't really gamble when they take a risk, they have looked at the pros and cons, and decided the pros outweigh the cons to take some action, as their intuition tells them it's a calculated risk worth taking.

THE RISKS WORTH TAKING

Being prepared to take a calculated risk is entirely part of the key to success. Following that inspired idea with some kind of action…by us. This combined with the self-discipline to see our plans right through to brilliant conclusion.

I have started a few businesses over the years and not every single one has panned out as I would have ideally preferred, but that's called learning and yet I know the responsibility for this is entirely down to me for not having always payed due attention to the clues before me in the past.

I can tell you for sure that virtually every active participator in life will have gone through similar learning experiences at least once or usually quite a few times in their careers. The trick here is to carry on anyway, straight on to the next opportunity and with a little bit more wisdom on how to not do it now handily stored away.

FIND YOUR MOTIVATONAL STATEMENT

All the successful coaches I know use (and advocate to others) the adopting of motivational mission statements to create a clear idea of why they do what they do.

We all have a mission in life, the one thing we are meant to do that is our role to fulfil in this world. Okay, to give you the complete picture, this can change throughout our life and it is possible that what is our mission in one decade might evolve into something entirely different a little further down the line – but for now let's work on finding your primary mission in life. You need to be able to sum this up on one short easy to remember statement.

Here's mine…

We are all capable of way more than we ever imagined possible and all that untapped potential is waiting right there within us ready to be released…

It's how I live, and all my actions take me further towards realizing my mission.

Give some real thought to your own motivational mission statement, this matters precisely because it will define you. Have it as the home-screen on your phone/computer, print it out and keep a copy in your wallet, leave yourself post-its where you'll see them often and you might like to keep a card with your mission statement right above your bed taped to the ceiling. Anywhere you're going to see it often.

Your Motivational Mission Statement needs to be highly memorable to you – to embody you. Then repeat it as a mantra until it positively seeps from your pores, as you absolutely live and breathe it!

MY EXPERIENCE

This book is not about me, it is about each of you and living whatever success might mean individually to you. Having said that, if some of my own story or indeed those I have helped, can lead to a clearer understanding, it is useful for me to share. I have changed the names of anyone I do use to illustrate points.

As in my workshops, I share with you what has worked for me or often more usefully what didn't, who or what has inspired me and what I have learned about why some people succeed while others don't.

I am going to use the term Energy (short for Life-Force Energy or chi, that power we put into action whenever we think or do anything at all) when describing the forces of cause and effect that govern our life, our interaction with the larger world or Universe. This term is certainly not intended to replace any deities or the god which are an integral part of anyone's belief pattern or system. Although I fully respect any belief system or religion that harms no others, I feel it makes it simpler for what we are aiming for here to think in terms of the energy exchanges between our own thoughts and wider world or indeed others, if it is described this way.

4

DEFINING SUCCESS

Choices
Always a choice…always a choice.

The concept of Success is incredibly personal to each and every one of us.

Success being many things to many people; you or I do need to be sure to take the time to define just what being successful means to us personally:

1. For some this will be doing exactly what they love every day and getting paid to do so, the actual amount of money is irrelevant, so long as they can pay their way, all is good.

2. Others will think it terms of a financially rich lifestyle, freedom to perhaps travel or live somewhere they always wished to. They perceive a rich lifestyle for them isn't necessarily about

literally possessing millions; it is more about being able to comfortably do everything they wish to and having the freedom of choice.

3. Or success can mean literally having millions in the bank, ten houses, a yacht in Monte Carlo, helicopter, their own private island and a Mercedes in every colour of the rainbow.

4. Alternatively, living off the grid in a hand-crafted hut, surviving off the land and rejecting the concept of money all together!

5. Buying a campervan to tour Australia and write a travel vlog on the way.

6. Or any another entirely personally inspired scenario that nobody else might have yet even thought of…

Ponder deeply as you focus your attention on your perfect utopia, your perfect vision of your own life as you have always dreamed it ought to be. And be honest with yourself here.

There are no rules when it comes to where our life can go and isn't that rather awesome? Nobody said everyone's ideal reality of success needs to be the same…find yours and that is what you aim to live!

> **Success is in your hands, your life to renew**
> **Taking the action to live dreams is down to you**

HIRING NOW!

Guess how many entrepreneurs first went and studied business at University? Hardly any at all that I personally or indirectly know of. Instead they got out there into the big wide world and learned for themselves on the job.

I am not being down on education here; obviously it is extremely important, especially for specialist subjects like accountancy, medical professions or law.

I have had many Uni graduates come along to see me for interviews over the years armed with their business studies or psychology degrees; and they fail to impress me solely because they are packing a big degree. In my businesses I have always been more interested in the enthusiasm of a candidate, their ideas and how well they will add value to the team.

Personally, I don't care if a candidate has first class honours degrees in business management, if they shake hands like a damp dishcloth, fail to look me in the eyes and can barely raise a smile on their face they are not going to find their way into employment so easily. Not with me anyway!

KNOWING WHEN TO QUIT

Sometimes you have got to know when to quit, turn away from that particular dream and close the chapter in the most mutually beneficial way. Some businesses have simply run their course and the industry quite literally no longer exists – a prime example of this is the trade magazine business I grew over fifteen years ago, the emergence of the internet as most traders' primary source of purchasing rendered paper trade publications entirely obsolete.

The same framework applies if we are employed by someone else. If the prospect of getting-up each morning is kind of dreaded as it means yet another day of doing something we fail to buy-into or enjoy…then it's time for a long overdue career change. We will get to this all-important subject a little later in the chapter Discovering Your Talents on page 191. You might like to carry on reading in the meantime, rather than jumping ahead though, as it won't make too much sense without first absorbing the information between here and that future chapter.

E-COMMERCE

As I have moved into full time writing and seminars, most of my business interests these days are built around the internet in one way or another.

E-shops and online bookstores reach markets a high street shop or even personal business website never could – well not without spending a few hundred thousand a year on advertising. I write books, record audio books and go out into the big wide world to give talks - I focus on what I love to do.

I do appreciate how fortunate I am. I get to make a difference in the experience others have in their lives. Yet I know in reality what I do is show others the latent potential they always possessed within themselves but didn't quite know how to apply in their day to day life.

BUY INTO IT 100%!

Buying into your own dreams allows others to as well…

If you want your ideas and dreams to get taken seriously, the candid truth is YOU need to take them seriously first.

How important to you are those changes you want to make in your own life?

Are they a priority?

Can you get passionate about them?

Do YOU believe in your own goals being achievable?

Walking our path to personal achievement, in whichever area of life this might be, with others also buying into our vision of how amazing life can be increases the fun factor tenfold and absolutely lends much appreciated extra supportive energy to the process of getting there.

Can you imagine how crushing it would be to have your significant other, family or your circle of friends telling you that you are wasting your time attempting to move on in life or you would be better to stay exactly where you are?

If your goals don't consume much of your imagination and focus, if they don't seem exciting and even a little scary…then it is time to find a new dream which you can feel like that about!

CARING ENOUGH

If you don't care, how is anyone else supposed to care either?

It might seem like the easiest choice in the world to not care, after all you're never going to be disappointed if you decide nothing matters.

Yet…and yet what do we set ourselves up for?

The paradox here is by not caring we are setting ourselves up for disappointment after disappointment, until unfortunately this becomes kind of the accepted normality for us. Learned helplessness.

Caring about our own life, our own future path, requires commitment and for sure, although life may well still present challenges (it is how we grow as people) caring will ensure we find a way around, over or through the issue before us. And the reason is because we care to care, this involves us directly in the process of creating our own amazing life.

Would you rather choose being passive as you observe everyone else moving on in life and having all the fun? Or instead decide to be right there in the driving seat of your own life and be the one making awesome experiences happen for yourself?

Free-will dictates there are always these options...I know which I prefer and my whole motivation is to show others those choices, to let them hopefully also decide to take the fun option!

5

THE THIRD THOUGHT

A desire all fellow humans see
Potential for all they can be.

Although many of us can initially have every intention of carrying through a plan or working towards fulfilling a long-held dream, for the majority people it doesn't quite end up playing out like that.

More often their thought process, the inner conversation in their minds, of far too many people goes something along these lines:

THOUGHT ONE - A brilliantly original idea comes along, often spontaneously popping into their mind, perhaps when they awaken in the morning or maybe observing something in passing inspires them; and naturally they are engaged and excited at this point.

THOUGHT TWO – Okay, so next to do something about this amazing inspiration and for a short while their mind works overtime on different positive ways this idea can happen for real. Practically getting from where their idea is now all the way through to its magnificent realization consumes their attention.

THOUGHT THREE – They gradually start to have an inner conversation of limitation. To begin to persuade themselves of how to maybe not have it all happen after all. Their inner conversations now start to convince them it was a poor idea anyway and far better to stay put in their safe Comfort Zone (Trap) because this is always the easier option.

This is The Third Thought in action, which does single-handedly stop more potential winners from achieving their dreams than anything else!

How many incredibly pioneering inventions or life changing innovations have been lost to Third Thought limitation we will never know.

You or I have always had the freedom to live beyond The Third Thought, these inner conversations of limitation, and instead take control of our own destiny. It has been there waiting within every one of us. Listening to our intuition and then taking some kind of action each and every day is the key. Naturally, I will talk much about self-empowerment throughout this process and then you can live truly limitless!

THE THIRD THOUGHT SOMETIMES WEARS A DISGUISE

The Third Thought is our inner safety catch, it keeps us locked-out from doing anything outside of our usual experience.

Excuses for inaction and self-distracting displacements bought-into rather than instead taking some action are ways The Third Thought acts upon our lives. There exists a myriad of such displacements, each ultimately taking us further away from fulfilling our potential. All the time we get locked into these we are passively falling into the comfort trap of The Third Thought.

Are we filling our subconscious with those rich experiences to help take us all the way to the top or focusing instead on self-limiting displacements?

There always exists a myriad of tempting displacements, each ultimately taking us further away from fulfilling our potential. All the time we get locked-into these, we are passively falling into inaction or worse still, stopping all the good stuff we would love to welcome into our lives from ever manifesting!

These come in many forms:

1.   What we choose to read alters the way we perceive life. Whichever form our reading literature takes adds to our subconscious mindset. Children often act out the characters from their comics, we are certainly the same. As a youth I read spy novels and for sure, they influenced my thoughts and behaviour at the time – anyone I saw wearing a tuxedo was obviously a spy, with a hundred concealed gadgets about their person! If the first thing we do every morning is make our breakfast and then work diligently through a newspaper to see who is killing who and which celebrity has fallen from grace this week, what kind of a day do you imagine we are setting ourselves up for? Our choice of reading matter subconsciously informs our opinion of the world. Reading personally inspiring literature daily vitally helps keep us on-track.

2.   Television and the cinema. What we view on television isn't called a programme for

nothing. Everything we watch on television or in the cinema is passively programming us with usually fictional dialogue and images created by other people we don't even personally know. By the way, rather alarmingly our subconscious does not know this experience is fictional and treats this input exactly the same as any real-life experiences. Rule of thumb here is would we personally wish to hang out with those characters we invite directly into our lives via television or in fact engage in living their kind of life? If we spend more than 4 hours a day watching television, imagine what we might alternatively do with those 28 hours each week, the 5 days lost each month or even the 60 whole days spent each year watching other people do stuff? Imagine how amazing it would be to use those 60 days to be actively creating a brilliantly more fulfilling life instead! How much further forward might you personally be right now if gifted two free months to pursue your dreams?

3. The internet can be wonderfully informative and enlightening. At the opposite end of the scale, the internet can misinform and take us

further away from our goals. I can go set up a vlog right now offering advice on how to service the braking system on a truck, I mean I know less than nothing about trucks or how they stop, yet I am free to go ahead and give my uninformed opinion to anyone who cares to listen. Vigilance is constantly needed to ensure the accuracy of the online information many others are taking as accepted fact.

4.   Music creates feelings. The energy it gives off directly affects the cells of our body and minds. This one has been scientifically proven. Ponder for a moment those famous experiments which have conclusively shown how music affects the wellbeing of plants in a positive or negative way, then think how it might also affect the more sophisticated form of life known as you. So many of us download music directly into our heads by wearing noise-cancelling headphones. If your pleasure involves listening to music which actually has pretty negative messages in the lyrics (and you know exactly the type I am talking about here!) sorry to have to tell you that you are dramatically self-limiting your potential by directly programming your

subconscious mind with trash! I am not suggesting here you go and delete your entire catalogue of music if you are into thrash-metal, emo bands or whatever; but you are definitely doing yourself a great favour if you buy-out of listening to it all for at least a week to see if you feel any different.

5. Addictive computer games such as those with brightly coloured quickly moving images designed to keep us playing on, are also keeping us from doing things to change our life. You know the score, we are talking here about the ones widely marketed via television and pop-ups or sidebar adverts on websites, enticing us all to join in the fun and carry on playing to reach infinitely ever higher levels.

6. Mobile phones have revolutionized our daily routine; yet if misused they are as addictive as sugar and those people who are spending every waking hour playing games, texting or taking selfies for social media are not only living a fantasy life, they are also failing to live their dreams.

It is all down to what we want from life. That word choice again. Personally, I choose to spend my days in constructive pursuits - writing or giving talks to help others; and spending my down-time furthering my own personal growth or enjoying life enriching experiences, moving my life forward. Many others choose otherwise. Reading motivational literature, listening to uplifting music and using our phone more as an actual phone allows us to keep right on keeping on all the way to our goals becoming our life.

Okay, a question – would you rather sit by to watch others have all the fun as they gradually embody their idea of utopia **or** instead get personally active in creating for yourself outrageously expanded expectations of all YOUR life can be?

If you know for sure that you personally buy into any of the self-defeating displacements and limitation inducing distractions, how about you allow yourself a **Personal Empowerment Experiment?**

THE PERSONAL EMPOWERMENT EXPERIMENT

Spend three days without buying into your personal choice of distraction/s.

If you take hours devouring every word of a daily newspaper don't buy it for three days, leave the TV turned off if that is your thing, avoid the internet if you usually spend practically every waking hour on it, if your pleasure involves listening to music which actually has negative messages in the lyrics (and you know exactly the type I am talking about here!) don't do this during the experiment, play no computer games if they usually take your attention and finally use your phone only for essential communication if it is usually your life.

- The first day is going to feel extremely unsettling as you take on a completely different daily routine.
- The second day will more than likely see you constantly craving the missing element from your life. Go ahead and stay with the experiment anyway, after all only one more day to go!
- Day three though will be different. Look at what you might do you don't normally have the time for. What action can you take right now to start making a few positive changes in your life? Read something enlightening or motivating, see what college courses exist locally or online, go talk to some interesting contacts or even begin to meditate or have a go at yoga. Anything at all you

don't normally allow yourself to do because you are far too busy and don't have the time.

Life will change, priorities will change, and this can only be beneficial in the long term! To YOU.

6

WHAT ELSE STOPS SO MANY FROM ACHIEVING SUCCESS?

Determinedly she continued her endless quest
Grateful to know the mountain, deeply blessed.

FEEL THE PAIN

There is another way in which individuals can limit themselves and this is the fear of pain!

We are not talking here necessarily of actual physical pain, although in some cases it can be, it is more in terms of those achievements in life worth having are sure as anything going to require some type of direct action and effort on our part. Old established mindsets will have to be discarded. New mindsets leading to new experiences.

The martial artist who wishes to attain that elusive black belt is sure going to have to put in the hours of toil and sweat to finally arrive at that honour. Any mountain climber will confirm the path to the summit is rarely straightforward. The brilliant musician or artist will have spent many years perfecting their craft.

Yet all these people and indeed all those who rise above the masses in any other field of endeavour, will tell you it's all about the journey. The ultimate outcome is inevitable, and they will be fully aware of that.

For them it is the living in the moment, the satisfaction of perfecting their actions which is its own reward and choosing (and it's always a choice!) to enjoy the path, the journey to their ultimate destination - fulfilling their dream.

This Zen way of looking at life
"It's all about the journey"
...takes us far

Engaging with living in the moment and caring to enjoy the process, whatever twists and turns life takes, will ensure continued adherence to the path and arrival at your destination.

There may well be mistakes made (it is usually how we learn how to not do something), there may well be some tougher days to endure along the way...yet for all that there will also be those times of amazing achievement and exquisite beauty to enjoy.

LIVING FOR THE MOMENT

A question I used to ask at some point in my seminars succinctly sums this one up:

Me "What time is it?"

Cue everyone looking at their watches or phones.

Me again "Oops, too late! By the time you looked at your watch or phone the moment was already gone"

It's always NOW! This is the only constant. Now.

Everything else is simply either past or future tense.

TO QUIT OR NOT TO QUIT, THAT IS THE QUESTION

With apologies to Shakespeare for this sub-title, it is nevertheless a fact that no book or seminar can do the work for you.

It is also a fact that out of those reading this book not all will make it to the final page. Once some readers realise this isn't a magic potion to automatically transform lives with no personal effort, the real changes coming from how you or I persistently apply this information day in and day out, they will choose to quit.

Which is all as it should be. You and I cannot absorb what we are not yet ready to apply or fully comprehend and this equally applies to any area of personal growth.

Back in 1991 I first left the comfort (or as I saw it confines!) of the corporate world to begin my own learning curve and start my first business. With no real experience of the ins and outs of the true commercial reality of running a business, I slightly naively assumed the keys to success were mine to impart to all who cared to listen!

Off I went full of confidence to share my message, little realising I had only taken my place on the first step of knowledge. With the benefit of nearly three decades more experience I can look back to smile at my frequently misplaced over-enthusiasm in those days. And yet had I not taken that first step I would never have reached the point I am at now.

For sure though, if I ever found myself foolish enough to believe my learning was done I would immediately relocate to a small island with no phone or internet then I wouldn't be tempted to communicate my folly to anyone else!

Nobody can do it for us. It is what you or I do, the future we focus on and the action we take to get there which determines our own success.

CHANGES

We will get to dealing with and leaving Comfort Zones (Traps) shortly, before we arrive there though, it's worth mentioning that us humans are creatures of habit...

To radically change life for the better, however, certainly does not require us to radically change as a person. Quite literally all that is needed is a shift in our awareness of what can really be brilliantly possible from life, then consciously choosing to go out there and make that possibility our reality.

This simple shift makes all the difference.

There is nothing at all wrong in feeling trepidation at the possibility of change, it is natural to fear the unknown. This fear of a change in our lifestyle is great actually, it means change matters to us! Indifference would be of far more cause for concern, fear is the sign here we are doing something we deem important.

What this entire process aims to do is place your future directly into your own hands, then any changes are measured and intentionally calculated...by YOU!

7

WHAT DO YOU THINK?

Please help open my mind. Rationality limits potential
Quieten pointless ponderings. Let my mind be free

IT'S ALL ABOUT ENERGY

Everything in The Universe is energy, even the air we breathe and the water we drink is composed of atoms combined with energy. Thoughts are also energy, this has been proved by quantum science. Therefore, you or I are quite literally what we think. What we focus on creates our reality.

Of course, constantly attempting to monitor all the many millions of thoughts we have each day is utterly impossible and quite possibly the fast-track road to madness!

What we can all do though is remain vigilant of any self-limiting patterns in our thoughts which might be us attempting to persuade ourselves to stay right in The Third Thought, rather than getting out there and actively engaging with life.

What we constantly think about affects firstly our own self-image and consequently, how we are then perceived by others. Our thoughts (and words) also directly influence our actual physical wellbeing and mental health.

The cells of our bodies are constantly being bombarded with thoughts and crucially the emotions behind those thoughts. There are the thoughts of ourselves and like it or not, the thoughts of those around us. And our bodies and minds listen to these messages (and words) it receives loud and clear, reacting accordingly – regardless of us being consciously aware of it. For sure it can all be different though…really different.

Therefore, we are all creating our very own version of reality every single second of every single day. What we think, feel and say via our personal energy wave is making the reality of our life!

Yet more paradoxically if we care to listen to those words of others, when they voice opinions about us to our face, to a lesser degree it will still affect our inner and outer well-being, depending quite literally upon how much credence is given to their point of view!

Energy reacts to the messages we are sending out, our own personally projected energy wave and helps us to become our own idea of how we look and the life we lead. For better or sometimes unfortunately for worse; thankfully it is entirely possible to change this for ourselves. Beginning with a few remarkably simple adjustments in mindset.

Feeling good about YOU is vital for success and living beyond any possible self-imposed limitation!

By shifting the emotions behind what we think and focus on, we possess the real power to transform our own lives. If we passionately feel we are a success or a failure, then either of these will be the life we lead.

The words we use have an unimaginable power to control our lives. Here we are presented with one of the easiest of all ways to help overcome any false self-programming we might have unintentionally inflicted upon our own life. We will come to the power of words in due course, for now though...

THINK OF PEOPLE YOU KNOW

Do those who moan and complain all the time come across as brilliantly happy examples of humanity?

Or the professional cynic, expletively going through life mocking others and exhibiting sarcasm, do they seem full of joy?

Are those who fixate on illness usually healthy?

At the other end of the scale, how about those teachers at high-school who always seemed to have a ready smile and were encouragingly inclusive with the pupils in their class (perhaps you met at least one of these educational gems on your journey through school?) they rarely had to discipline students, and everyone felt better for attending their lessons. Or the neighbour who is genuinely interested in what we might have to say, never gossips and laughs along with our jokes, don't you feel good for passing a few moments with them? These guys are happy people, sure they have their share of issues like all of us, yet they choose to face the day with a smile and pleasant words.

TAKE RESPONSIBILITY

A vital part of evolving and growing is coming to an acceptance that the things which occur in our life or happen to us, are the responsibility of us and us alone. Our thoughts, our own actions created the reality you or I are living right now.

Your own life happens <u>through you</u> or in other words you are the pivotal point around which the whole of your life experiences occur.

Life, when analysed, is ALL about choice.

We make choices every hour of every day, and the resulting reality of life we then lead is a direct consequence of those choices. These are **our** choices and there is nobody else to blame if we end up becoming dissatisfied with the outcome of those decisions we made. It is up us to then make different choices and change those decisions which sit uncomfortably with us.

Even deciding to make no more choices, to just deal with whatever life throws at us…is still a choice!

It has become quite the trend to blame others for the parts of our life which we find don't quite suit us. Apparently, it is all the fault of the government, parents, neighbours, the education system, that guy we work with, our partner, bad luck, todays horoscope or perhaps even aliens!

I am sure you will agree it is time for us all to collectively wake up and make a long overdue reality check in that cop-out way of thinking. You or I attract into our life situations via the choices we make and energy of the thoughts we put out (and as we will see later, the words we use to describe our life and ourselves).

The moment has arrived to let go of any self-defeating or limiting behaviour. Accept the personal responsibility for the reality of our current circumstances, using them as a springboard to create bigger and better things.

Think deeply about this and you will see the truth in this reality.

WHAT RELEVANCE DOES THIS ALL HAVE FOR US?

So, we are all quite literally what we think. Physically, spiritually and very much manifesting materially.

The other aspect we need to consider here is we ALL listen to this constant stream of thoughts going on in our own heads. Our own conversation with ourselves.

How can we be sure every single one of these thoughts or inner conversations of ours is genuinely true? For sure, we quite naturally tend to believe what we think all the time. Accept it as concrete fact.

How about this one though…

When you were sixteen years old (assuming you are not sixteen now) did your set of belief patterns, what you were completely sure life was all about, match exactly with the way your belief patterns work right now?

Yet at the time, at sixteen, you were sure your thoughts were 100% correct and believed them to be the absolute truth about yourself and the world around you.

Our truth evolves.

Learning to meditate can help a lot here. Later through our journey meditation will be covered. Most fellow coaches I know or know of, advocate using meditation and I consider it an essential life skill we can all benefit from for multi-layered reasons.

How many times have you gone against some inner feeling to forge right ahead with a course of action you kind of knew at some instinctive level wouldn't work out well? I admit I have also been there, done that and for sure it seldom has a great outcome!

We need to buy out of believing every single conscious level thought we have, our inner conversations, and automatically assuming them to be correct. Instead **developing trust in our intuition or gut instinct if you like**. This bypasses those conscious-level conversations we all constantly have with ourselves entirely; and frees us to usually make the right choice.

It is these inner conversations which lead to us staying in Comfort Zones, because it's easier. Well actually it isn't easier at all, leading as it does to feelings of frustration and lack of control of our destiny. Yet many of us do manage to convince ourselves to stay right where we are, rather than make a leap of faith into something new, to see where saying YES takes us.

Our imagination is one of the most powerful assets we possess. And has practically nothing whatsoever to do with logic or rational thought.

8

THE POWER OF THOUGHTS TO AFFECT HEALTH

A thousand random thoughts vie for attention.
Only the chatter of mundaneness. Never did mean anything.

There is an old saying - image, ordain and manifest.

In other words, think about something deeply keeping that image strongly focused in your mind. Then say it out loud and the energy wave transmitted makes it happen for you. And it still holds 100% true.

Phil's greatest fear was losing his mind! Having witnessed his much older brother succumb to dementia, Phil dreaded the horror of his own life following a similar path. Although he was perfectly fit and led an extremely active lifestyle, unlike his retired brother, he nevertheless fixated upon the unlikely chance of developing a certain illness. For sure his brother had passed away through this illness, however, this hardly compelled Phil to also go ahead and experience the same fate. Especially given his radically different lifestyle. By fixate I mean he read everything there is to know about the subject, often verbally expressing just how much he did not want to get the illness or lose his mental faculties. And sure enough he did eventually find his life turned upside down. Phil didn't get dementia, sadly though he did develop an inoperable brain tumour. With only a few short months of life ahead of him, Phil did finally have the chance to make the connection between the thoughts of fear he had vocalised for years and where he now found himself. Did Phil's thoughts attract his illness? He was certainly convinced they had.

At the other end of the scale, the energy from our own thoughts can bring about little miracles.

A woman I know cured herself of the arthritis that was supposed to kill her physical body before she turned thirty-five years young. After her rather depressing diagnosis, with promises of agonizing pain confined to a wheelchair and apparently having rather less than five years left to live, she followed her gut instinct and completely changed her thinking and diet. This while

74

also dealing with the unfortunate reality of her best friend succumbing to precisely the same fate and passing away from advanced arthritis some less than six months before she got her own diagnosis. With absolute single mindedness, she took up meditating and yoga. She changed her diet, switching to eating almost only pure, unprocessed food. Letting go of a considerable amount of emotional baggage she had been carrying around with her since childhood; becoming far more at peace within herself in the process. Finally confronting and dealing with the grief of losing her best friend and the more than likely guilt-driven self-planted subconscious expectation of succumbing to the same illness herself. Some thirty plus years later I am happy to say that my mother is still very much alive and kicking (and never ended up in that wheelchair).

WHAT DO YOU NEVER WANT?

Well, for sure, there is one proven way to attract to us the things we don't want and that's to constantly think about not wanting them. And tell everyone around us how much we don't want them. The energy of our thoughts works the same way always. Like Phil, who became convinced he had caused his own illness to manifest.

What we think about all the time, what we focus on, what we talk about – all becomes our reality, and this includes all those things we don't want to happen, which we put so much energy into not wanting.

So, if you or I are spending all our time focussing on and talking about stress, depression or feeling unwell, for sure, that will be the reality of our day to day life!

INDECISION SENDS OUT A POWERFUL MESSAGE OF LIMITATION

What we think about constantly creates our reality, in every single sense, every single time without cessation. And this does work equally well with the things we fear, just as strongly as it does with those more positive experiences we would rather attract into our lives.

Yet, there is an upside here! The rather cool reality about all those negative thoughts is that if we wish for something to not happen, it does take rather more effort than wishing for some positive outcome instead. And does take rather longer to manifest as well.

For sure constant vigilance is needed, there is some good news though.

The upside is that clearly here has to be entirely possible to completely change our lives by simply changing our minds, what we focus on.

Thinking about what we DO want, keeping our focus positively and fixed on those results we actually desire to happen.

Keep our thoughts good and positive life will always be interesting, for sure there will be challenges (it's how you and I grow as people!), however, with a more positive attitude within our thoughts and the power of words or how we choose to verbally express ourselves which is vitally important, we can live a harmonious life.

Expectation does create the life that we live.

9

EXPECTATION CREATES RESULTS

Raising our standards.
Expectations of amazing outcomes!

Bill Bolton's reputation preceded him. Coming across his company through the wholesale business I ran for over a decade, in the trade Bill had unfortunately attracted the generally accepted reputation for being grumpy, cantankerous and abrasive in his way of dealing not only with customers but his own staff!

Yet I knew Bill and I might have a mutually beneficial business relationship. Having talked to him on the phone, I also sensed perhaps Bill chose to be so un-user-friendly as a kind of armour, a defence mechanism against the world.

Making an appointment to visit his premises I decided as I parked my car I would treat Bill like he was the most friendly and pleasant man I had ever been fortunate enough to meet. For the next hour I reacted like I hadn't noticed his scowl or sour demeanour. Instead I smiled and behaved like he had brightened my day purely for being in his company. Eventually he simply had to start reacting himself more in harmony with the open, friendly way he found himself subjected to. To the shock of his staff Bill even laughed at a joke he had himself made at one point!

I bought a few items from him, securing a discount without even needing to haggle. Over the next few years I would visit his warehouse once a month, Bill made a point of dealing with me personally and we did become as close to friends as I think he found it possible to allow himself to be. He would drop me an email if he thought he had found an item he knew would be in my area of interest.

My expectation did indeed bring us mutual success. Rather than believing his reputation, instead I chose to treat Bill as a fellow human I was delighted to meet; and I think to his initial surprise, he found himself reacting in kind to me.

BELIEVE IT CAN HAPPEN

If you or I ever really want to achieve anything new and amazing, then we need to firstly unequivocally believe it is possible for it to happen! It needs to become as natural as opening your front door, you put that key in the lock and you are home.

Belief is the unwavering inner knowing that what we need can genuinely surely happen. We might not yet know exactly how it's all going to play out, although in truth the physical details are unimportant. The important part is the belief it can and preparedness to take personal action once the moment arrives to show itself, as it surely will.

TAKING ACTION

Nothing interesting ever happens in the life of sedentary people.

For us though, first comes the expectation of results and secondly some clear action which needs to be taken to be able to bring about whatever we desire.

After the genuine expectation (Energy), then later comes our part of the deal to fulfil and 99.9% of the time it is going to require the leaving of Comfort Zones (we will finally confront comfort zones in the next chapter) and getting directly, personally involved with the ultimate outcome.

Once you have been working for a while with consciously projecting your Energy, it becomes second nature to become aware of the time arriving for action when it makes its presence known. Then is the moment to truly come alive and invest those actions with a nice healthy dose of enthusiasm and passion. Together with the thanks and gratitude you will naturally feel for another dream becoming the reality of your life.

The man who had a vision to revolutionize production line technology, Henry Ford once said something along the lines of "If you think you can or can't do a thing, you're right"

INTEGRITY

Being a person of our word is vitally important. When making promises ensuring we can fulfil the commitment made. If for some unforeseen reason, circumstances change and render following through on a promise impossible, explaining how and why to whoever it affects in ample time before the allotted moment of fulfilment. And if possible following through at the soonest opportunity later.

It goes without saying if we wish to be taken seriously, considered trustworthy and respected, we need to behave with impeccable integrity. Keeping those words we say together with our actions, honest and open to scrutiny by anyone.

Having made the decision to live your life with integrity, you must be honest with yourself first and foremost. Have there ever been any occasions relating to your past behaviour where perhaps you've sailed a little close to the wind, like been economical with the truth for personal gain or to avoid the consequences of your actions?

If this is the case, that's awesome, the fact you are honest enough with yourself to accept this is brilliant. And what next, is it time to move on and leave it all behind you now? Well, almost…

If you have this kind of past, then know for sure that you are going to be tested. Do you genuinely possess the kind of integrity you are projecting now? Or is it just skin deep? Situations occurring allowing you to show your true mettle and your resistance to the temptation of falling back into those old comfort zones.

Being a person of integrity may not always win you thousands of friends, it is certainly going to attract the right one's though!

10

COMFORT ZONES OR TRAPS!

To stretch comfort zones. Be in The Zone
More changes yet I am constant. Life changes, I grow.

Public speaking had already become second nature to me, I felt (and still do) a buzz of excitement of pure joy stood before an audience ready to communicate. This will always be an inherently two-way communication. I know my own story inside out, I sure prefer to know yours and then I might help you more effectively.

Poetry was different though. The prospect of laying myself creatively on the line, publicly sharing my poetry for the first time did lead me to question my sanity more than once as the date of the evening literary festival approached. I felt compelled to do it all the same, if only to once again walk the talk I had been telling others for years about relating to leaving our Comfort Zones!

Ironically, as I arrived at the venue on the night in question the organiser came to see me backstage and asked a favour. Having already attended one of my **Naturally Stress Free** talks, he knew how I usually function in front of an audience and so asked if I might mentor two nervous first-time performance poets to let them share the stage with me and then they would feel more at ease. He assumed, as a regular on stage I knew what I was doing and equally assumed I must have performed poetry many times before. All my own concerns forgotten, of course I said YES to his request.

And us three went on stage together that night, to stand next to one another at three microphones, with me in the middle to lend them a little extra sense of security. I introduced us, performed a poem, then led my new friends into their own performances, us then taking it in turns to share our creative endeavours. It was great fun and for half an hour I believe we managed to entertain our audience. Well, they applauded at the end and before that laughed at the right moments, so chances are they enjoyed our poetic tales.

The organiser did me a great favour that night. Without realising he put me into a mindset I felt 100% comfortable with. Mentoring others, helping them to find the inner confidence to leave their Comfort Zones, resulted in me not even considering my own any more. After all mentoring is my stock-in-trade, it is what I do! My own misgiving completely forgotten, out I went personally feeling like I had been performing poetry for years…and that is exactly how everyone perceived me.

Mindset in everything and the apparent limitation of a Comfort Zone might well turn out to have been a mirage after all, once you or I choose to do something awesome and embrace one of those slightly scary new experiences.

COMFORT TRAP!

Comfort Zone as a descriptive phrase leads some to falsely believe here is a delightful place to be, they are wrong – it never is!

Life begins beyond a Comfort Zone every time.

There is a world of difference between living each day feeling comfortable with life, satisfactory daily progress being made towards our goals and the other reality of existing trapped within a Comfort Zone. For sure our

Comfort Zone might more accurately be described as a Comfort Trap, as this so aptly fits exactly the way it traps us into static inaction and indecision.

A Comfort Trap does us no favours at all, projecting a sedentary self-image and more tellingly leads to inner frustration, developing this underlying sense of the futility of life.

Clearly then what is needed is a way of escaping that Comfort Trap and getting us out there into The Zone instead.

The Zone is the place to be, this is where quick, exciting decisions are made, and equally exciting stuff happens!

Have you ever experienced, if only for a few moments, being right there in The Zone?

Do remember how it felt? Thrilling, focussed and every sense heightened…

The Zone is that state of being which usually entirely by-passes our thinking mind; instead we tend to react more in an instinctive, following-our-gut kind of way.

To arrive at existing within The Zone, rather than any comfort trap (I refuse to give it capital letters from this point on!) is going to require we make a fantastic leap of faith. Knowing that whatever comes along once we are out there on our way, is only going to strengthen our resolve and make the end-game ever more worth the effort.

BY CHALLENGES WE GROW

There is a common misconception that being happy means having no issues or challenges to overcome. Nothing is further from the truth! Overcoming challenges and triumphing leads to wellbeing and happiness way beyond everything running smoothly every single day.

We learn nothing from routine, it's out there making changes happen for ourselves and coping with the curve-balls we occasionally get dealt where we truly grow. More importantly every time one of those challenging type of situations is encountered we discover exactly what we are brilliantly capable of and there is truly a win/win situation to celebrate!

Okay, getting to where you or I wish to arrive can either take the shortest time or in some cases practically several years. Wherever we are headed though, once we leave that confines of that old comfort trap our journey has begun and for sure life is about to suddenly take on brilliant new meaning and our days will get one whole lot more interesting.

START IN A SMALL WAY

Is there something you might have always wondered what it was like to do, but your falsely self-imposed limitations apparently rendered it impossible?

This can be from practically any starting point.

In my case, ever since my early childhood I had possessed an irrational terror of large ships. Tracing back through my own timeline I realised this originated from a children's picture book about The Titanic and other shipwrecks. Bizarre, yet true!

Finally, about fifteen years ago I chose to undertake a day-trip on the very source of my fear. A large passenger ferry to visit France, in quite rough seas as it turned out to be on the day – only to leave myself with no other alternative but to have to repeat the journey in even rougher seas in reverse coming back home late in the evening. Sure cured me of that one!

You can do the same with anything similar in your own life and mentally tick off another supposedly impossible task completed.

My first boss instilled in me from day one (when he had me rather tentatively phoning potential customers to pitch within an hour of arriving for my first day at the office) it's fine to make a few mistakes, that is the only way to learn. And oh boy did I ever do exactly that with those first few phone calls! After a week or two though I began to understand what to say and how to say it to get a higher percentage of the positive responses rather than those turn-downs.

CONSTANT IMPROVEMENT

Constantly pushing back the boundaries of what we are capable of, improving each day in however a small way, refining how we function within our living and working environment is a magnificent way to live. These tiny adjustments each and every day are outstandingly self-motivating.

As one who has spent years daily looking at how I might do things better, I can tell you not only does this add to our success mindset it always ensures we feel inspired to achieve more.

> **Even if you feel trepidatious about something you are contemplating undertaking for the first time, go jump right in and learn as you go along.**
>
> **None of us are born experts, this only comes through experience!**

Take any action at all you can to break down those self-limiting imaginary barriers we can all carry around with us, however small to begin with. To start off with this might even seem almost trivial, for example:

1. A fear of sampling new, unknown food.
2. Discomfort around animals.
3. As I had, fear of large ships.
4. Fear of wearing any colour other than black (I know someone who had that comfort trap and now she says how liberating it is to be able to wear any colour or pattern she chooses!)
5. Or even fear of paper books! Apparently, this is a growing issue in year one at schools and assuming you might be reading the digital

version of this book or listening to the audio, please feel free to help yourself (and my book sales! Win/win again) by ordering the paper version.

Doesn't matter what it is, however trivial or random it might seem, every time a small but well-entrenched comfort trap is overcome it further validates the fact bigger ones can surely also be taken-on and left in the past...right where they belong.

A significant part of really living life as it is meant to be, is a willingness to push on regardless of the fear which might well-up inside us, those inner conversations of doubt trying to persuade us to stay-put. Carrying right on without becoming paralysed with indecision or in other words buying into The Third Thought by talking ourselves out of action – life is all about choice (as we will discuss many times throughout this process)

Rather than being a spectator, choose to be an active participator in life.

Jump out of that old comfort trap to confront that mirage of a limitation head-on! That compelling sense of inner satisfaction is incomparable.

And go through the process once, next time around it is going to be palpably easier. Start small and break down that first comfort trap, then move on to another.

Imagine waking each morning full of excitement for the coming day, loving how you spend your working hours and chilling in the evening feeling deeply satisfied when looking back over the happenings of the day. Sound good? This can be YOU!

11

HAPPINESS IS ALL ABOUT YOU

*Happiness from deep inside
then at last you are free!*

Being happy seemingly comes easily to some fortunate people. No matter what happens within their life they constantly seem to have a smile planted firmly on their face and a pleasant demeanour most of the time. Naturally these individuals rarely lack friends and are wonderful to be around. Their happiness being entirely contagious!

Too many of us seek some outside force or material things to feel a sense of happiness…yet it is never to be found anywhere but right there within each and every one of us.

A new material possession can temporarily excite us and equally temporarily make us feel like we are happy. That feeling never lasts though. What you or I crucially need instead is a way of remaining happy…whatever!

IT'S A CHOICE, THAT WORD *CHOICE* AGAIN

Our inner conversations with ourselves, the ones we talked about earlier. These are the key to living a quality life and remaining fundamentally happy. Those facts about the world we hold to be true, the ones we constantly re-affirm through our inner conversations. And yet, as we have already proven with the example of our sixteen-year-old self, these truths do evolve and change.

Maybe our poor inner conversations about happiness might go something like this:

1. Well, you know, I need to deal with everyday life don't I, rather than all this theoretical stuff.
2. I'm always having to pay those bills, they never seem to grow smaller, am I supposed to be happy about this?
3. Don't even mention those stressful trips to the busy grocery store I must endure every week or

any of the other thousand and one hurdles that come along in life…

4. Life is hard sometimes and no amount of pretending it isn't will make it any better.

Can you or I remain happy and still deal with all those curve balls life may throw at us?

Yes!

Absolutely…

Living happy is possible for any one of us to achieve as a definite decision to take. There is a clear path to getting there and we are all free to consciously choose to walk it.

No matter what comes along we will be able to deal with it while remaining calm. Eventually getting to the point where problems are instead viewed as challenges which are there to be happily overcome, rather than these horrendously unfair random happenings for losing sleep and to worry over. In fact, **happiness is our natural state and it is now long overdue for us to collectively reclaim this birthright.**

It only needs for us to take on an easily adoptable new mindset, as we shall see…point of fact it's remarkably simple yet will usually require leaving the comfort trap of a previously limiting mindset we may well have been falsely holding on to for far too long…

ACTIVE SMILING

Look at yourself in a mirror and pull a face that is comically glum. Next smile at your reflection…it is like an instant face lift!

Here is the start of an exciting different approach to life and one which is going to turn out to be seriously fun (how else?).

Each morning while you are looking in the mirror, getting ready to go out and experience your new day look yourself in the eyes and smile. Keep smiling for at least a minute and wish yourself a happy day.

If being serious and grumpy can unfortunately often become habit-forming for too many, equally so can smiling and being happy.

How about making smiling your new hobby? **When you first waken up in the morning, when you first open your eyes...smile.**

During the day, if you feel stress starting to make itself known and tension builds up. Step away. Take a few moments out and go to the washroom. In privacy smile and keep it up for at least a minute, tell yourself out loud or if you prefer in your mind, that you are happy and will easily cope.

Every time we practice active smiling not only are we re-programming ourselves to have a different outlook, we are also happily creating happy endorphins in our brains and these act on our nervous system...making us feel even more happy.

Although at first, we may well feel like *acting* like we are happy, eventually and surely, it is going to arrive at the point where our both conscious and subconscious start to believe the messages of happiness they are being constantly subjected to and we can become our own wonderfully self-fulfilling prophecy.

Triggers anchoring us to stay happy are useful. Here are some of those triggers, use them, buy-into them and watch how your attitude to life changes:

1. Perhaps there are songs or a genre of music that inspires and lifts your moods? Play it often.
2. Are there certain colours you find uplifting? Wear them and surround yourself with them.
3. Walking officially lifts our moods, if you feel a little down or lethargic, go take a walk.
4. Conversation and interaction with fellow humans can be incredibly uplifting.
5. As is being in love and feeling loved.
6. Enjoy reading? Read inspiring books or stories, expanding our knowledge about something we are interested in must make us feel better.
7. Go smell a rose! Seriously, if you have a local park or perhaps a garden of your own, take the time to inhale the fragrance of a rose in full bloom, the heady scent can only lift anyone's mood.
8. Crosswords or mind puzzles such as Sudoku are not only calming, they have the added benefit of brain-training as well!

It is easy to be enthusiastic when things all seem to be going well for us, how about in the more challenging times though? Those moments when there seems to be a chain reaction of all that bad stuff happening. **This is the time to really come alive and shine!**

ENTHUSIASM AND YOU

Don't feel in the mood to be enthusiastic? Well then act with enthusiasm anyway. It may be only acting, but I can tell you this for sure, do it often enough and you will have created a brand new you.

Crucially by getting ourselves into the habit of firstly only acting and thinking positive, we are bringing enthusiasm into life and the life of those who know us. People are going to notice and react to us differently, in a far more positive way. Creating the rather cool by product of consequently making us feel and react in an even more enthusiastic way.

Suddenly you are way more employable as well; everyone loves a person who's enthusiastic. If you work for yourself, unwavering enthusiasm for what you do takes you all the way to where you desire to be.

You will have become that type of person who embraces life and shakes it about to see what fun can be had.

Others will gravitate towards you as your attitude inspires them. And really, what could be more perfect?

BY THE WAY

Absolutely avoid making any important decisions if you are feeling stressed, unhappy or under duress. Wait until things are more settled within your emotions, then tune into your intuition to feel which is the right choice.

12

YOU DESERVE SOME QUALITY YOU TIME

She only had to look within for comfort
Then was the time to become still

Stepping back from our daily life and the world at large on a regular basis is incredibly rejuvenating and good for the soul.

If possible going somewhere closer to nature or if that is unfeasible, at the bare minimum away from the usual environment we live/work in. Finding a quiet place to preferably not even think at all and simply be. How magical an experience this is for all who choose to just be alone and feel for once who they truly are! Perhaps for the very first time…

If finances or circumstances don't allow a solo vacation this is not a problem, instead take one day a month to retreat from others. There is always going to be a way in which this can be made to work to a greater or lesser degree, although greater would clearly be preferable, of course.

My own life is usually nicely full, my schedule in a typical week sees me writing for magazines, taking part in interviews to talk about my writing or giving one of my own talks. The way I have of finding some battery re-charging time is to take myself off for an all-day solo coastal walk or deep down into the forest. This is especially effective in the heart of winter when the harsh weather discourages many others from venturing outside. It is a challenge in this era in which we live to find some true seclusion. I have to say though, a gale force wind and driving rain usually means I am going to have the beach pretty much to myself – and with the magical bonus of making me feel wonderfully alive, leaving me with a heart full of gratitude for nature in all its extremes.

Take the time to take some time out for you – there is always a way.

SOMETIMES PUTTING OTHERS FIRST

Stay with me here, this isn't quite the horribly glaring contradiction to the previous section it might appear to be at first glance.

There are those times when selflessly doing things for others makes us feel so magically amazing inside it has to be good for the soul. In fact, although we all definitely need time-out purely for ourselves if we are to function to the maximum of our ability, acts of kindness for others are truly beautiful and it is often the small things which make a major difference to others.

There was a trend started over three decades ago and popularized by amongst others the late Princess Diana, of practising Random Acts of Kindness. This might take the form of leaving books where others will pick them up for free, paying for the car behind at a toll-booth, making eye contact and giving a genuine smile to someone doing a mind-numbingly menial job, buying a meal or blanket for a homeless person or even paying for the groceries for a housebound elderly neighbour without them asking and having them anonymously delivered as a "gift" from the store. How about we collectively make Random Acts of Kindness once again go viral as they did in the mid 1990's?

105

Obviously giving of our time and love to our family and friends is pretty much a given. On a wider personal level putting others first can be letting someone else have the first drink of communal water when on a trekking adventure. Easily letting the person who has only one item to buy go before you in the supermarket queue or voluntarily giving freely of your time and devoting it to helping others. Any of the thousands of ways our actions can make another person feel wonderful and happily consequently ourselves as well.

It has even been said that helping others is a purely selfish act for the great returns we get in terms of how it makes us feel deeply satisfied as well. So what? Are you or I not allowed to also derive pleasure from the process? For sure we are absolutely supposed to feel great as well. Caring and giving of ourselves must be all round good medicine then!

13

FREEDOM FROM THE PAST

Precious life. So many things to do.
New horizons. Opportunities to grow.

We all want to experience more times where we feel good rather than bad, yes? Yet how many of us can honestly say this is how our life plays out every day?

Let's see what we can do to redress the balance.

An essential process allowing us to be free to live the life you or I deserve is to practically let go of any emotional baggage we are quite unintentionally carrying around like an invisible weight on our shoulders. And paradoxically many of us are seldom aware we are even doing this!

Our reactions and behaviour are informed by our past, those emotional responses when a similar scenario occurs. If this takes us further away from our goals or seems illogical (even to us!) the time has come to resolve the issue and be free.

THE WAY WE FEEL AND STRESS

Our feelings act like a barometer. The way we feel about a situation or indeed an individual gives us invaluable feedback about our stress levels relating to that exact thing or person. This is how our feelings react like the gauge on our internal barometer. Some feelings will make us feel pleasantly sunny, then again others more like a grey cloudy winter's day.

In a very real sense the emotions that we feel about anything tells us rather usefully the effect the situation or person is having on us right now. Even if this is from long ago in our timeline, when pondering the situation, those feelings inform us of how we still view the event or person.

EMBRACE OURSELVES

Clearly then it is only natural to want to have only those good feelings and buy out of all the bad feelings, right?

Well in the long term yes, but first there is a process we need to go through, one which will allow us to experience outrageous freedom and self-knowledge!

Those things we feel good about when focussed upon are those ones which don't require any work. We are perfectly happy with the situation and we need to treasure those moments, those things we feel good about. For this exercise we need to then collectively put them metaphorically to one side for now.

Next, we need to focus our attention on our bad feelings. These bad feelings are far more useful to us when wishing to deal with any latent stress about the remembered person or event from our past, which can now be brought forth and dealt with.

Point of fact, there are not any genuinely good or bad feelings. Feelings are invaluable feedback. Our bad feelings are to be appreciated, as these show us areas of our lives that we need to work on, areas of our lives we now need to change.

Feelings are energy. Our own personal energy. And as we already know, the energy we project creates our own version of reality. To grow and maximise our potential then we vitally need to free ourselves from anything at all within the way we feel which might limit us in any way from being all we can be.

Fine, so now we know those areas of our lives we feel worse about, the poor thinking energy, happily there are clear strategies or actions we can take to be able to transform that.

UNRESOLVED EMOTIONS

These cause blockages. These blockages manifest through feelings of futility or frustration within the way our own life functions. Another unfortunate by-product of these emotional blockages when undealt with is that they can lead to genuine physical illness or depression.

Overcoming emotional blockages is to overcome our own set way of looking at firstly ourselves and then the outer world. Our interactions with everyone and everything in our life, based upon our built-up experiences and standard responses.

All situations occurring in which we react by own set-up well established rules and yet seem to take us further away from our objectives or make it more difficult for others to see our point of view, are based on some long distant occurrence in our past. Or in other words, learned behaviour.

WE ALL SET RULES FOR OURSELVES

Rules on what is acceptable within our own behaviour and also that of others; and often these rules can be quite rigid. At one time in our life they may have been perfectly reasonable and worked within our framework for us right then. We are creatures of habit unfortunately and by being creatures of habit what worked for us when we were say fifteen or sixteen years old, certainly won't be working for us in exactly the same way when we are instead forty or fifty!

So, you or I need to look at anything in our lives which is self-limiting us. Any of our own self-made rules about what is acceptable or unacceptable.

Really deeply ponder this, dig-down forensically to examining all the individual rules you make for yourself and especially any of them which no longer seem to be serving you.

One of my own rules for life which I felt delighted to let go of about twenty years ago, had once seen me relentlessly going through my daily routine in precisely the same order every day. Why exactly would I do things this way became the question? After all, one of the foundations of all I teach is to be flexible and open to change. Eureka! Now thankfully every day is different, I still have tasks I want to perform, yet by mixing everything up more randomly, my own personal engagement in what I am doing is maximized. By never buying-into a set routine ensures my approach is fresh and I remain awake to any opportunities which open before me.

Examine any of your own set of rules. Once we have done this, then it is time to let some rules go. You are going to feel so much better…you will have to trust me on this one! Make the effort to do it for yourself right now and see!

Jane felt uncomfortable with compliments or any time a significant date in her life came along, such as a birthday or anniversary, she felt overwhelmed when receiving gifts and told me she just wanted to run away from the situation. Clearly, she had underlying issues, ones which were preventing her from fully enjoying life and led to those closest around her; her husband and children frustratingly failing to understand why she always reacted in such a way. Digging down into her childhood revealed she was one of six children, Jane being the middle sister of three girls. As the more responsible of the three sisters she had always looked out for her baby sister, as there wasn't too much money around, anything Jane received over and above her basic needs being met (occasional foodie treats, gifts or new clothes) she would invariably share with her sisters.

The household was run like a military academy; with six children, her parents considered imposed strictness as essential for everything to run smoothly. Not surprisingly Jane felt more than a little starved of love and attention. There was a siege mentality inbred into the children, and Jane would consistently place her personal interests last to share what meagre things did come her way with her sisters.

Working with Jane over the course of several sessions got her to come to terms with her childhood and see it more in perspective. That her reality today was informed by her experiences growing-up and the guilt led feelings of somehow being unworthy of love or nice things happening for her. Forgiving her parents, realising here they were there dealing with the reality of six children, all crammed together with them in one small house, and on an extremely limited budget. As parents this must have been mighty stressful at times for them and imposing discipline in the way they had was just their coping mechanism, allowing them a sense of feeling a little in control, when so often they didn't. Letting go of the situation through understanding a childhood situation through more informed, adult eyes, finally freed Jane from her childhood guilt created emotions, to feel way more at peace when nice things happen to her now and thoroughly enjoy the experience.

We do also need to address phobias, fears and misplaced anger to free ourselves further. And all these will have their root in some, often long consciously forgotten incident which happened directly to us or we witnessed.

PHOBIAS

If you live with a phobia, think about when you first really experienced it, where in your personal history did you become aware of this reaction? What age were you?

If you have a fear of spiders, as a small child did you witness someone else reacting in fear at the sight of a spider?

Same with a fear of flying, perhaps you once saw photos in a newspaper or saw an incident on television what featured a plane crash? Maybe you even overheard a conversation or documentary questioning the safety of

GO PLAY BALL

Freedom to be free…and it has nothing to do with sport!

We can all possess that persistent thought or poor-thinking mindset we are fully aware doesn't serve us and we would rather let go of. That limiting thought pattern which comes back to haunt us whenever a similar situation occurs, or we endlessly ponder any poor life choices we might have made and re-live those times we felt ourselves being treated unfairly by another. If you are experiencing a little difficulty in feeling the love when letting go of negative situations from your past, how about possessing the power to do precisely that in your own hands right now?

Wouldn't it be just a little awesome to leave all those limiting thoughts and mindsets exactly where they belong…in the past?

I have good news. You and I can choose to do precisely that. And it can happen in a moment!

LET'S PLAY BALL!

This ball game may have absolutely nothing to do with playing sport, but it does have everything to do with discovering a new-found freedom to live on our own terms.

You are going to need to find somewhere quiet, far from any possible disturbances or distractions. As you begin to focus all of your attention on just one troublesome thought or self-limiting mindset. However painful it might be, you really do need to FEEL the pain associated with the thing which is bugging you.

Now comes the fun part!

Imagine wrapping the thought within a ball, placing it right there inside the ball. Now this can be any kind of ball which speaks to you, the actual type isn't important – soccer, rugby, tennis, basketball, whatever. The only given here is that the ball has to be hollow inside.

See that troublesome thought now sitting right there inside the hollow space in that ball.

So how about we get rid of that thought forever, banish it from ever returning?

Sound good?

Let's do this!

Kick, throw or hit that imaginary ball with such force that it travels massively rapidly vertically upwards. Really give all your energy into sending that ball straight up into the clear blue sky...and the magical part here is gravity has absolutely no effect on the ball whatsoever!

Up it carries on, gaining momentum all the while, quickly passing out of your sight...until eventually it hits the upper atmosphere and you see a brilliant flash of light as it burns away, together with the thought contained within it. To never return to earth or you...

SUMMARY OF WHAT WE JUST DID

This is a subconscious-clearing exercise I first developed in the mid-1990's and immediately applied to my own life at the time. Then later sharing it with those I have helped over the decades has validated the effectiveness of this simple visualization. Feedback from others has confirmed using this method brings incredible freedom to leave behind literally anything at all which might possibly hold us back within our own mindsets.

We can practice this method on as many self-limiting mindsets as we choose. The only rule is one issue at a time and only one per day. By all means use Play Ball to clear your subconscious as many times as you sense you need, but you do need to leave a gap of at least a few days between each session (a whole week is ideal) to allow yourself the opportunity to integrate your transformed mindset into your life…to see how things work differently for you now. Experience has shown Play Ball does bring often dramatic shifts in attitude and feelings.

Once a week, on a set day is ideal to clear each issue by Play Ball. I found using this exercise every Sunday evening set me up beautifully for the coming week.

It's like a spring-clean to the subconscious!

ACCEPT THE GIFT

What if a person you were loosely acquainted with, from your extended circle of friends, out of the blue offered you an all-expenses paid holiday of your choice and all you needed to do was choose the destination and turn up, how would you react?

How about a distant second cousin randomly deciding to gift you a brand-new car? What then?

Moving closer to home, how do you feel when your temporarily unemployed friend insists he wants to stand his round of drinks or you receive an unexpectedly generous birthday present from your elderly relative who relies only on her pension to live?

With the law of energy or chi taken into consideration there is one answer and one answer only. Smile as you graciously accept the gift and be happy for the generosity of the perpetrator, for surely their actions in due course are about to bring about many good happenings in their own life.

To react in any other way, You or I are treating ourselves like we are somehow unworthy of good things happening. Please re-read this chapter several times to put into practice these self-releasing methods until you feel differently.

We DO deserve good things happening in our lives. Irrespective of what we may hear to the contrary, it is our birthright to deserve to feel good…be happy!

To allow for the good flow of energy, any freely offered gift and this can equally take any form such as giving of time, listening rather than talking or even a literal item, has to be cheerfully accepted and with due gratitude. Any other course of action is interrupting the giver's personal energetic flow of attracting good things via the actions of their own energy and you or I certainly don't have the right to do any such a thing.

Always feel comfortable with accepting a freely given gift and develop the habit of feeling infinitely happy for the giver's generosity, as for sure it will boomerang straight back into their life at some point and probably in their near future.

You might like to also get into the habit of freely giving kindness to others for creating mini miracles in your own life.

DAILY EMPOWERMENT ROUTINE

In the morning, before you start your day, take a few minutes to think of a few things you can feel some passionate gratitude for...then keep that passion with you as you go through your day.

Last thing at night do the same, focus on your goals as you fall asleep. This is programming your subconscious to work on your terms, to give you the life experiences YOU want and attract those things into your day which help you travel all the way to your goals becoming your reality.

14

THE COMPANY WE KEEP

They thought that they could rain on his parade
Thinking he listened to any of the points they made.

Or to put it another way, the people we choose to hang-out with!

Next, we need to deal with quite a large elephant in the room.

Although this is quite widely known these days, yet often not really taken seriously enough, the main five people we hang-out with are those we end up coming to the same level as socially, emotionally and economically. Clearly then, our crowd can either help us or hinder us, it all depends.

I always did my best to get an appointment somewhere far away to avoid attending the office end of year party and yet never seemed to quite manage to! This is back in my corporate days and as head of a department, attending this big annual social event was an obligation (but not if I wasn't there!).

Frankly I found one or two of my fellow publishing movers and shakers bleakly challenging to spend too much time around. Usually during the year, I would be out on the road four out of five days, being at this party though inevitably brought me into close proximity with those very people I tended to quite easily avoid the rest of the time. This was in the days before smoking inside of restaurants became banned by law and this event would see me spending several long hours listening to expletively ridden moaning about how bad life at the office is or else slightly drunken self-aggrandisement, all whilst simultaneously peering through a thick cloud of cigarette smoke as I attempted to make out who I might actually be talking with anyway. All in all, a thoroughly grim experience.

I have ensured over the years with my own businesses to surround myself with happy positive-minded people. And equally importantly made our work environment a fun place to be – and definitely no compulsory to attend end of year party!

THE UPSIDE

We will have all met those fabulous gems of people who make us feel great about ourselves just by being in their presence. Then there are those friends who, no matter how long since we last enjoyed their company, spending time together again you always seem to slot straight back into the friendship, conversation easily flowing like you have never been apart.

Sadly, not everyone we meet in life always has quite this harmonious effect. There are also those individuals who are, let us express this kindly, more challenging to be around.

LET'S MEET THE DREAM-STEALERS

You all know the type. Those prophets of doom who can only see the negative in everyone and everything. The unfortunate individuals who make the brightest sunny day seem damp and dark, only for some time spent in their doom-ridden company. These dream-stealing people love nothing better than to rain on our parade. And although quite often they never seem to achieve a great deal in their own life, they do nevertheless consider themselves ideally qualified to judge us, advise us and attempt to quell our enthusiasm for where we are going in our own life.

If you think about it they are rather like a living, breathing manifestation of negativity in human form. Now, of course, these people have issues going on in their life, like everybody else. What this does not mean to say though is we are also required to buy-into their issues.

Choose our friends wisely, then they can help us along our way, as surely as we would assist and motivate them when needed. Good friends can be a true inspiration and I am sure we would all wish to be that kind of friend as well.

Taking it as established fact that you or I really wish to grow as people, as discerning individuals we need to take some time-out having an impartial look around our own circle.

And then calmly walk away from those dream-stealing stress-inducing acquaintances who make it feel like an hour spent in their company lasts a fortnight! Feel free to send them love and compassion tenfold if you sense you ought. Just for the sake of our wellbeing we definitely need to **avoid hanging-out with them at all costs!**

HIGHER FRIENDS

If we do end up coming to the same level as those we are pleased to call friends, how about seeking to make friends with those possessing greater knowledge or those brightly shining high-achievers within whatever our chosen career path might happen to be? Having such friends engenders within us the often much needed aspiration and motivation to encourage our inbuilt natural desire to evolve. Stretching our limits to become greater. Competing to become the best version of who we are is, of course, the only race worth getting involved with. Yet, our brilliant friends can contrastingly show us many truths about ourselves and frame our potential.

Brilliant friends are those who never judge, seeking the same things from life as us, purely to evolve and be happy.

NEGATIVE PEOPLE ARE THERE TO TEACH US

How true.

And those challenging people who enter our lives all have something we can learn from and how often it is all about ourselves. Wonderfully poetic, if you think about it, after all how else can it possibly be if we are to grow beyond being a victim of circumstance, to take the power back to control our own lives – including most importantly buying out of the stress associated with dealing with these types of people.

For sure, if we choose to, we can attract a wonderful circle of amazing friends and indeed more intimate friendships. We need to treasure anyone who falls into these categories and our role is to mirror their qualities back to them.

If the people we are surrounding ourselves with are negative thinkers, it is going to have a knock-on effect to our own mindset. **We need to raise our standards. Raise our standards about who we choose to spend our time with and give our attention to.**

So, how about those extremely unpleasantly behaving individuals we all occasionally encounter? Are we meant to tolerate their company regardless of their frequently shocking words or actions? The lessons the particularly obnoxious behaviour of others can teach us is that their actions are unacceptable, and we deserve better. We need to raise our standards, it is ours (and indeed their path) to disassociate from one another.

Some people still have bigger lessons to learn about themselves, their nasty behaviour is showing forth their need to address their issues and deal with them. This certainly never compels you or I to become a part of the daily drama of their life or put up with disrespectful treatment. Buying-out of this type of individual's negativity can literally be the lesson to be learned here. It is a matter for our own self-esteem, our standards, confidence – to be able to calmly let their vitriol wash over us, walk away and then promptly forget all about it!

The opinion of these self-defeating, highly negative people is seldom what is seems. Any hurtful vitriol (which is poor thinking in essence) directed towards us is of practically no importance whatsoever. Unless we allow it to be. Buying into their viewpoint by validating ourselves or defending our position, gives their opinion the power to control the way we feel. Their mindset is informed by their own experiences, you and I are just a handy target by being in their vicinity.

Assuming we do not agree with the negative statements made about us to our face (and I sincerely hope you don't!) simply let them go, as their statements are totally invalid and irrelevant. Our reality is different, and now it is time to move on in peace. Let them have the freedom to evolve at their own pace or not. It's their choice.

127

If we do occasionally need to come into contact with people like this and we just let it all wash over us, then walk away when we can do, for sure our stress levels will drop dramatically!

ADDICTED TO DRAMA

What we also need to take on board is some of those people we encounter are addicted to drama in their lives.

Through this understanding, whenever you or I encounter such a toxic person, we can choose to see their reactions and mindset more in context.

Drama addicts are going through life running a subconscious programme set to chaotic situations. And if life isn't giving them enough of their default setting, unfortunately they create it for themselves…

This is actually never about us, by the way. Whenever encountering such an individual, we bring ourselves much inner peace by choosing to buy-out of any of their negative behaviour. To view it more accurately as this person is consistently creating this reality for themselves wherever they may go and more than likely with whoever they are in close proximity to.

On a subconscious level confrontation is constantly what the drama addict seeks, even though it clearly makes them unhappy. Choosing to remain calmly detached, rather than giving up our centre by getting angry or trading insults, allows us to retain our personal power.

We cannot teach anyone knowledge they are not yet ready to learn, there is little point in saying too much to a drama addict about their self-defeating poor thinking mindset, rather better for us to focus on living on our own terms and let them evolve at their own pace.

In every case showing by example works more effectively than verbally attempting to show the drama addict how self-defeating their mindset is.

15

GRATITUDE IS ALL ROUND GOOD MEDICINE

Accepting all that crosses our path. Seeing it as it truly is. Another grateful opportunity for growth.

Some of us go through life focussing solely on the things we don't yet have. Feeling that once we have acquired those desired material items or achieved all the success we wish for, then we can at long last give ourselves permission to feel happy and fulfilled. The kind of life where once a certain level of achievement is gained, only then can we allow ourselves a sense of gratitude for what we have attained.

This is a great pity.

Let's bring out just one more time for posterity the extremely well-worn phrase **Gratitude is the Attitude**.

Maybe these days this sounds like a terrible cliché as it has been used so often by so many and perhaps even losing a little of its impact in the simplicity within which it explains an eternal truth; and yet if you or I put this into daily practice, the reality of our own life will take on a whole new meaning!

Gratitude absolutely attracts more things into our lives to feel grateful for. This alone ought to be motivation enough to focus on what we already have and what appreciation for it might do for our quality of life right now.

Everyone, in every single walk of life has at least one thing to feel gratitude for and this can be down to even the most basic of our needs being met:

1. Like clean water to drink, food to eat.
2. The beauty of a genuine smile given freely.
3. To look around as the warming sun shines down or observing a flower resplendently in full bloom, at the other end of the scale, crisp white freshly fallen snow which has yet to walked in.
4. Witnessing a sunrise or sunset.
5. An interesting conversation shared with a passing someone and this is before we even get

to thinking about friends and family, those we love or feel loved by.

6. Having a place to live or enjoying time with our pets.
7. Those experiences which have helped shape us into the person we are.
8. All the thousand and one things in life that some of us can wrongly take for granted, whereas in fact we need to instead look at with gratitude from the bottom of our hearts.

We need to able to appreciate what we already have.

Passionately appreciate who we already are, right now, even though we may well possess the deepest-rooted desire to grow as a person. We all need strong foundations to build upon and active gratitude ensures this is the case.

The only way to achieve all the magical things we have the potential for is to be grateful for what we already have and practice active gratitude every day.

If you currently own a beaten-up old car, feel grateful for the way it takes you where you wish to go and be sure to look after it just as if it were new. Gratitude for your current wheels ensures your reality of owning a new car moves so much closer to becoming true.

ACTIVE GRATITUDE

Make it your habit when first waking up to be thankful for another day and the opportunities it can bring.

While you are looking in the mirror brushing your teeth (that early morning bathroom mirror again, for sure this is the best possible time to programme how our day will unfold) getting ready for the day ahead, look yourself in the eyes and think of all the things you ought to be grateful for, even down to the most fundamental of your needs being met, like the fact you even have the mirror to look into or that toothbrush!

Make it fun and enjoy feeling grateful. If you can laugh and smile all the better, positive emotions carry the message of gratitude via our personal Energy infinitely stronger. And what we put out there is surely what makes our life.

The more we can express our happiness and gratitude for what we already have…the more we allow greater and more outrageously wonderful experiences to enter our lives bringing us the naturally occurring self-fulfilling prophecy of being able to feel even more gratitude. Life is quite literal like that, the more we put good positive energy out…the greater positive experiences enter our lives.

What have you got in your life to be grateful for? Find something. Find lots and lots of things! And really feel that gratitude!!!

16

FEELING COMFORTABLE WITH SUCCESS

Trust intuition and it will guide you in the right direction for you.

We all know the stories of those people who after winning big on a lottery, a few years down the line are right back to square one, having quite effectively managed to spend all their new-found wealth.

Their unexpected good fortune found them completely unprepared inside (their success mindset) to really feel comfortable living within the reality of being a financially rich person. Internally they were still exactly where they existed prior to this windfall, their deeply entrenched comfort zone was one of limited options financially. Their wealth incongruous with how they had always lived, led them (consciously unintentionally) to ensure they quickly lost their money to take them right back into their comfort zone.

Ian is a perfect example to illustrate our point and how it doesn't necessarily have to be that way. Well, clearly for long-term wellbeing it is absolutely essential we do feel comfortable within expanding into our greater happiness, health and success. Anyway, back to Ian.

Out of the blue Ian found himself in possession of fifty thousand pounds as an inheritance he certainly hadn't anticipated coming his way. For years he had struggled to get by financially, he would gain employment only to then find himself quite quickly out of a job once more, largely due to his lack of self-confidence. And this pattern had been going around in circles for years.

Ian loved gadgets and tech. Within six months of his unexpected windfall he had already blown forty five thousand of it on all the latest electronic gizmos - yet found his life no nearer to fulfilling him in any way. He saw the prospect of a bleak winter ahead of him, and the likelihood of needing to sell many of his new toys to pay for the essentials of day to day living. Making a reality-check helped turn things around for Ian. Still possessing five thousand pounds we went through ways he might invest this to instead add long-term value to his life.

Off he went to College for the next six months taking an intensive business management course, to add to his skills set. Costing slightly under two thousand pounds, this still left him three thousand over to live off while he studied. He didn't need it all, familiar as he was for so long living a financially meagre existence meant his needs were simple, Ian found himself in the cool position for the first time of having some small savings in reserve. Armed with his brilliant new qualification and far more importantly a new found inner confidence, he commenced applying for jobs and quickly found permanent employment as part of the management team for a retail store. By realizing where he was heading (straight back into his old reality!) Ian invested some of his remaining cash into building his own financial freedom for his long-term future.

I have to share this other quick story with you! We had a family cat when I was growing-up, Fluffy she was called (because she really was very Fluffy). When not much more than a year old she hurt a front paw and for a short while limped. When sat she held her painful paw off the ground. I can't begin to describe how cute she looked with one paw raised like that and such a sad look on her face. Oh, and did she ever get sympathy - treats and cuddles came her way all day! Fluffy lived a long time for a cat, and thankfully she recovered from her poorly paw within a week or so. However, for the rest of her nearly eighteen years, whenever she wanted a little extra attention or a treat she would raise one paw off the ground and look sad. And what's more it worked every single time! Clever kitty.

Sadly, illness does also become the comfort zone of some people. Perhaps they subconsciously enjoyed all the extra attention coming their way when they were once unwell? We are what we focus on...

How many times do we come across someone who when we politely ask how they are, then proceed to tell us every single detail of every single ailment they are convinced they are burdened with?

Although we all experience those temporary moments where we are not functioning at 100%, we vitally need to focus our attention on ways to quickly recover.

Sure makes sense to me and I hope for you as well. Focussing on holistic wellbeing absolutely ensured my own recovery from a rather inconvenient health issue, I constantly pushed back the boundaries on what I might achieve by adopting different mindsets or refining my diet.

You or I need to apply our complete focus into being happier, heathier and more successful; and leave others to concentrate on limitation.

There are outrageously simple tricks we can all use to empower us to continually maintain a success mindset. Invest in you and watch your life change!

INVEST IN YOU

To get taken seriously by others we must take our own image seriously…

I was originally going to use the sub-heading Dress The Part here, but really that would be imparting only a partial truth. INVEST IN YOU is more accurate as it includes wider ranging implications, rather than simply putting on a cool dress or suit expecting that to do the work for us. As usual there is a bit more to it than that, what matters here is our whole mindset and those new neural pathways we are creating to hardwire our subconscious.

Feeling good about ourselves is crucially important and for sure an important part of this process is investing in how we present ourselves to the world and more crucially how that makes us feel…

Bottom line, if you are starting out and want to get taken seriously in practically any kind of area of business it for sure pays to look successful!

Wear clothes which suit the dream you are pursuing. When I first ventured out many years ago touring my Positive Living Talks, I decided beforehand that by wearing panama hats and positively psychedelic shirts I would stand out to get noticed - this certainly worked, gaining me much appreciated free press coverage at the time and beginning to put me on the map. Thankfully for everyone else I have moderated this with experience and now favour either a suit or a simple white shirt with smart trousers when delivering talks.

If we project successful, we are going to get taken seriously and actually become successful…isn't this a rather awesome self-fulfilling prophecy?

Dress to impress YOU first and foremost. Feel good about your clothes, hair and style, then you are projecting that the whole time and everyone you meet happily reinforces the feel-good factor for you. Buy the best you are currently able to afford, and you will soon have more spending power as your success increases.

Decide how a successful person in your chosen career dresses and take that purely as a starting point for inspiration, then develop your own style within this framework into one which is now shouting out 100% you.

If you are on a limited budget, you might like to consider how you allocate your spending. After you have seen to firm commitments, how can you make the rest of your money best work for you?

Invest any of your surplus cash into things which will add value to your life. This can take many forms including:

- Courses and further education

- Books

- Downloads

- Clothes for the feel-good factor

- Trips to hear motivating talks

- Conferences for networking

Anything at all, however abstract, which adds value to your life and brings those precious dreams so much

closer to really being your life is what we need to buy-into.

17

PASSION IS CREATIVE

Considering her journey in her own minds eye
Dawning realisation hit her, now she could FLY!

What have the enlightened spiritual masters from whichever religious doctrine they belong (or perhaps even don't) and all those materially successful self-made entrepreneurs got in common?

They are ALL equally passionate about what they are doing!

If we ever sense we might be falling into an old comfort trap of passiveness, renewed passion for what we do creates the most powerful energy possible and keeps us right there in The Zone!

We have the pioneers of quantum theory to thank for showing us the truth that all living matter is composed of energy which is interconnected. The greater Universe is also a manifestation of energy. As humans formed of energy, we interact constantly with this Universal Energy, even though many people are often not consciously aware of it. We are different though, in so much as we know our feelings, our emotions are a barometer of how we are looking at life. And we can most assuredly intentionally project our own energy to bring about those desired changes firstly within ourselves, and ultimately our day to day life.

BRING SOME PASSION INTO YOUR LIFE

By a series of slightly bizarre circumstances I found myself at eighteen years old managing the contracts department of a commercial publishing company. Given the chance by the managing director, who having followed his gut (always a good plan) offered me a three-month probation to see how I might get on.

I grabbed the chance and loved the job! I enjoyed the research to find leads, the travel and most of all I adored pitching to rooms full of potential clients – I wasn't to know it at this point, yet along the way I learned the skills required for communicating to large groups of people, those which I still use to this day.

146

Over my first eighteen months I brought an unprecedented one million pounds worth of new business into the company, while still a passionately motivated teenager in very much an adult world.

My successes lasted as long as I still had the passion for the process. Once I hit my early twenties, the routine didn't seem quite so exciting any more. Having already ticked-off every one of the boxes in terms of where I might take the job and visited most places here in the UK, I found travelling four out of five days to make profit for someone else had become tedious. As the novelty slowly wore off, my passion slowly wore off as well, inevitably a change of career beckoned.

I had instead developed this deep-rooted passion for running my own business instead, exploring my capability. I equally possessed a driven desire to also help others as well. In the early 1990's I stepped away from my first big success, with renewed passion to begin my journey to where I am now, and this will continue to grow further for sure. As I get more passionate about what I do every year, I guess I made the right call!

PASSION, PASSION, PASSION

Whatever achievements you or I wish to accomplish, if they are worthy of our time and energy, need to be invested with a large healthy dose of passion. Passion, together with the enthusiasm we discussed earlier, sure as anything makes any achievable change in the reality of our life way more likely to manifest.

Passion means absolutely believing in what we are doing. Here is something which truly matters and is worth making a resolute commitment to, for the long-term awesomeness it is bringing into our lives...

The sports person who competes firstly for the love of their chosen passion and although they may well get quite wealthy in the process it is never only about the money for them, instead their focus is on the challenge of exploring the outer limits of their physical ability. Those writers who simply must express themselves through the medium of books, they adore the art of creating words that flow or the public speaker who loves informing others to help them on their journey (that is my passion). The business person who can't get enough of doing deals; they live and breathe the negotiating process. The spiritual master who realises they know but

148

a portion of all there is and becomes like a small child full of wonder as the next wisdom is uncovered.

You know the score and I am sure you can think of more examples of passionate people. Perhaps you even know a few? Or better still maybe you are one yourself already? If not, you certainly can be by the choices you make!

WHAT NEXT?

Okay, we need to deal with another way some of us limit our potential to ask ourselves the question **why are many people unwilling to outwardly, publicly show their true passion for what they wish to do?**

Fear of failure and caring what others may think, judge or say if that happens.

If we dare to raise ourselves up to be observed, being passionate and enthusiastic, we are inevitably going to attract a fair amount of attention. Then come along those limited individuals who adore to ridicule or seize the opportunity to rain on parades, the dream-stealers we already met earlier.

If we are going to be judged anyway it may as well be for being a passionate and enthusiastic participator in life!

Yes, for sure the path to our goals may well take a few twists and turns, so what? At least if we are actively on that path we are going to arrive there some day and life will sure be interesting along the way!

Let's use any dream-stealer's negative feedback as a sure sign we must be doing something right, they would hardly be giving us their attention if we weren't and this is actually brilliantly motivating if you think about it.

I have always found this kind of attention a sure sign I am certainly doing the right thing and it helps keeps me right on track!

PASSION CANNOT BE TAUGHT

What we can all do though is find something within our timeline that we can get excited about. This may be from recently or maybe even in the long-term past, however, everyone is for sure going to have experienced at some point that overwhelming sense of passion and gratitude mingled beautifully together, the type that makes us feel happy to be alive. Buy into it to remember exactly what it felt like…

This wonderful feeling can be brought into other areas of our lives, tapping into the richness of passion and using that energy every single day to bring about a complete transformation in our approach to tasks.

This is an amazing freedom to enjoy life. It is okay to feel enthusiastic; it is okay to shout from the rooftops expressing the passion for what you are doing!

Furthermore, passion means that when things occasionally fail to work out quite as anticipated (which, let's face it, they sometimes don't.) We are surely going to keep on moving forward anyway and find another way. Look for that another way and there is always going to be one. Every single time.

YOUR BACKGROUND STAYS IN THE BACKGROUND

Whatever your starting point in life, passion and drive takes you places. Universal Energy doesn't care if you come from a family of twelve children with parents who struggled to put food on the table or were born into the most privileged of circumstances – your background is completely unimportant when daily living your goals. Having the clearest vision of where you are going, and a healthy dose of passion, is going to ensure you arrive. Energy is energy and works in exactly the same way for all.

Be passionate and you will gain much wisdom to easily live on your terms and, equally importantly, have one heck of a lot of fun along the way, as well!

18

ENJOYING A LONG AND HEALTHY LIFE

A simpler new life and his soul is at ease
To inner bliss and contentment, he has the keys.

Our human body is the chosen vehicle we use to travel around this bluey green planet of ours. It seems almost too obvious for us to then to take the best possible care of it and give our body the best chance to serve us well until the time to leave.

It makes sense then the fewer stresses we put on our physical body and digestive system, by choosing carefully what is taken into it, the easier time it's going to have.

I have found over the course of the last three decades that my own body reacts better to mostly unprocessed food. The more natural my chosen food stuff is, the smaller the list of ingredients on any kind of label gracing the packaging, the healthier and happier my body is.

Eating food free from artificial colours, flavour enhancers, e-numbers and preservatives means our digestive system is going to have an easier time coping with it.

EATING WHEN HUNGRY

Developing the habit of eating when hungry, rather than when the clock says it is a meal time. This is listening to the needs of our body and places far less stress on our physical system.

So many of us eat regular as clockwork and this can leave us feeling either hungry in those times when we are burning those extra calories or else overfull, because we ate when the clock said it was time for lunch, even if we didn't actually feel like it right now.

Grazing throughout the day, eating a little often, gives our digestion an easier time by never stressing it. Further on this subject, overburdening our body and this applies even to the healthiest food or drink if we overeat, is putting unnecessary strain on our finely tuned digestive system.

> **Take on heavy fuel, chances are we are going to get heavy.**

VEGAN, ANOTHER CHOICE

As someone who then lived the urban life, the invitation to spend a few days staying right in the heart of the country on the poultry farm owned by extended family was an opportunity I happily jumped at.

We seldom realise beforehand those pivotal moments which happen in life, this was to be such a moment.

Arriving late at night, the following morning I got the guided tour of the farm, consisting as it did of shed after giant shed of battery-hens. Entering the first of these sheds to witness first-hand the stark reality of confined life for the hens left me shocked and horrified. Over the next couple of days of my holiday I would occasionally venture solo to peer into the sheds observing more closely, but only from the safety of the doorway. If you have never seen such a place, let me tell you the stench and sound is overwhelming, that combined with the sight of tens of thousands of tightly caged birds ensured I left after a few days to return to my life now resolutely vegetarian and seeking to know more.

A vegetarian diet requires about 25% of the land required to feed a meat eater annually. For a vegan it is only 20%. Of two identical areas of land, one purely for rearing cows and the other given over to vegan food, the vegan plot will feed up to five times as many people. This crop will also require a minute percentage of the water needed by the cattle, and of course, none of the methane our bovine friends produce (adding to greenhouse gasses) are produced by that field of wheat!

Having graduated to vegetarian, I later graduated to vegan and am presently macrobiotic vegan, through listening to my own intuition during a recent year long journey to self-healing. I equally accept this lifestyle choice may be considered a little too extreme for some.

I do attribute much of my wellbeing to also becoming entirely free of sugar or artificial sugars in my diet. More of which shortly.

I drink plenty of water (but not too much) and get plenty of exercise. If I can't get out and take a walk (my favourite form of exercise) I do at least ensure to make the effort to have a 15-20-minute work-out with weights at home every day.

BROWN RICE

This has a bit of an image problem here in the West, I do get that. Brown rice has become a little synonymous with the tie-dyed hippie movement and free love. In the Far East, however, brown rice is an essential part of the diet.

And yet…

This ancient grain is one of the purest foods we can eat. Naturally high in fibre, brown rice still contains all the essential vitamins and minerals which get removed when it is processed to make white rice.

I hugely recommend this staple of a macrobiotic diet, totally regardless of your own dietary lifestyle. Brown rice regularly added into meal plans ensures you are taking into your body one of the most natural foodstuffs on the planet.

VITAMINS

We all have easy access to just about every and any type of possible vitamin, mineral or supplement conceived of or imagined. All we need to do is hit the high street or click a mouse. Yet how many of these vits do we genuinely need to be taking and how many are simply passing through our bodies serving little useful purpose?

During the last thirty years or so I confess, as a health aware vegan, I must have sampled at one time or another pretty much every of the myriad of different vitamin and mineral concoctions; the promised goal being to replace the essential elements vegans apparently miss out on through avoiding meat, dairy and fish.

The message here is vits are easily obtainable and we can all self-diagnose. If you do genuinely feel you could use some extra vitamins over and above your usual diet, take the time to go and get checked out by a health professional. That way you are sure only to be supplementing with something you need short term. Look at what can be added into your diet for the long-term fix.

If you are veggie or vegan, it is almost mandatory to have your B vits checked periodically as a matter of course and for peace of mind. A nicely balanced diet might well leave further supplementation obsolete. The other point to bear in mind here is that our needs are more than likely going to be entirely different during the summer months as opposed to winter; again, if your instinct is suggesting you would benefit from supplementation, a visit to your GP or choice of healthcare professional allows you to know for sure. Facts when it comes to our wellbeing are always preferable to guesswork.

JUICE

Five a day have become the watchwords when it comes to our intake of fresh fruit and vegetables. It is a generally recognised standard in order to maintain a natural balance in our diet, although more is always preferable to less and why only reach the bare minimum recommended amount?

Juicing fresh fruit and vegetables is an excellent way of increasing our valuable intake of their beneficial vits and minerals. Pre-packed cartons of juice we can pick up from the supermarket are okay, if there is no other option. To truly get a good balance of nutrients, juicing for ourselves is the way to go. Perfectly serviceable juicers have significantly dropped in price recently, becoming accessible for most budgets and the wonderful thing about juicing for ourselves is we don't need to add extra preservatives or any of the other stuff commercially produced juice often contains.

For more information about starting out with juicing combinations I recommend the book Juicing for Health by Caroline Wheater or something similar. Or finding a juicing website you can trust the validity of information from.

SUGARS

So, here we come to the subject of sugar (contentious section alert!) as I have mentioned this in passing earlier in the chapter, let's go talk sugar now…

Too many refined, artificial or even natural sugars, which are added to thousands of the things we choose to eat, is asking a lot from our bodies to absorb these alien substances which have only really become such a high percentage content in our diets in the last fifty years or so.

There is an excellently researched book called Sugar Blues by William Dufty, although written in the 1970's its relevance today cannot be understated. If serious about wellbeing I do recommend you read this or a similar book.

Sugar causes highs and lows in our moods. And so many of us are quite unaware of just how many refined sugars we are taking into our bodies every single day. Sugar is added to practically every single processed food. Even if you think you might well be having a low-sugar diet, check out all those ingredients and you will find virtually everything does indeed contain sugar or artificial sugar concealed under one name or another.

Sugar gives us a high. It contains no nutritional value whatsoever, but it surely does give us a high. That energy rush. Unfortunately, shortly afterwards comes the crash. We then feel lacking in energy, yet not only is it affecting us physically, it is also affecting our moods.

We met Jane earlier in Alive to Thrive having already dealt with her issues resulting from her upbringing, a year or so later she asked me for further help. She felt incredibly down and lacking in motivation a lot of the time. Digging down into her life revealed nothing of any real consequence which might be causing her to feel this way. I followed my intuition to simply suggest to Jane she might like to adjust her diet for a minimum of two weeks by cutting out as much sugar as she felt comfortably able to. She reported back after this fortnight she felt like her life had been transformed, experiencing a sense of being much more in control of her emotional wellbeing and balanced within her moods.

Really ponder sugar, research it online but first a word of caution. Be sure to read from reputable sources, such a lot of the online "research" on sugar has been rather sneakily funded by major soft drink manufacturers, not exactly unbiased advice!

Then if you agree with me, that sugar is not something which ought to be part of your diet – start to reduce your sugar level. Don't go cold-turkey and cut it completely out of your diet, gradually easing away from sugar will put far less stress on your body.

As part of my own healing journey I decided overnight to abruptly adopt a no sugar and free-from artificial sugar lifestyle. Convinced, as I personally was, that sugar had contributed greatly to the issues I found myself dealing with left me with little choice, I had to go cold-turkey. Having experienced this particular rollercoaster, I can tell you that gradually reducing our sugar intake is for sure the gentler way of doing things!

If you too go sugar free, you are going to soon feel the difference in your life. There will be a period of withdrawal, stay with it anyway and persist until your body is cleared of all the processed sugars.

I wake in the morning energized and have the most amazingly balanced moods/emotions I have experienced at any time in my life. I am much more at peace within myself, and you can be as well.

ORGANIC

There is organic produced food and then there is ethically produced organic food.

Some of the animal waste based organic fertilizers, such as chicken pellet manure, commercially used by growers and directly available to us via garden stores, has been produced as a by-product of factory farming in one form or another. This might be okay for many people; however, with the broader picture of ethics taken into consideration, feeding our plants with the by-product of a brutally efficient system of farming can hardly help us to grow happy botanical specimens,

The same applies with pesticides. Rather than drenching our food in chemicals, there are more natural ways of doing things. Permaculture is one example, the planting of sympathetic plants to protect one another from likely pests. Using essential oils such as citronella as a repellent to avoid crops being eaten by insects or lavender to discourage weeds are becoming more widespread. There is a wealth of reliable information on the internet from organizations such as The Soil Association and some version of the Organic Consumers Network exists in one form or another in most countries.

If you are buying most of your foodstuffs in from grocery stores, a little personal investigation into where their products come from and how they are grown can pay dividends. Alternatively, growing your own fruit and vegetables puts you in control of what products go onto them and happily there is a wealth of ethical organic options out there, either for fertilizing or pest control. We are what we eat…

SELF-INFLICTED POISONS

Many people do pay small fortunes in order to self-inflict pollution upon their bodies.

These come in many forms:

- Smoking, I am a bit of a non-smoker, well okay, I have never felt inclined to even try it. I am all for freedom of choice, mine has been to avoid tobacco. It has been known for certainly all my lifetime that smoking is hardly beneficial to health in any way. On the contrary it can create as a by-product, its own range of serious problems and issues with the ingested carcinogens. It would be highly presumptuous for me to suggest to every reader of this book they ought to stop smoking, but it would be wise if they did. I believe we are all responsible for our own actions and in these times in which we live, everyone is fully aware of the health risks involved in choosing to smoke. If you are doing everything else right and still smoking you are making your body work so much harder to clear the associated toxins. Cigarettes do also contain sugar, this surprises many people, they can indeed have a very high sugar content. Clearly the health hazards needing to be considered relating to a high sugar intake as well!

- Alcohol is often considered fine in moderation, some health experts even going so far as to suggest that a glass of excellent quality organic red wine or pure organic beer is actually beneficial. A rule of thumb here is if we avoid overburdening our body with anything that requires a recovery time from eating or drinking we are going to be pretty much on the right track.

- Junk food is not called junk for nothing! An occasional junky indulgence our bodies can just about cope with. Living off the stuff constantly is, needless to say, pretty self-damaging.

- Deep fried food is universally recognised by health experts as increasing the likelihood of heart disease, high cholesterol and diabetes. Again, moderation or avoidance must be the sensible option for all of us.

- Recreational drugs offer an artificial form of escapism. Far better to live the kind of life where you get high from living your dreams and feel excited to get out bed in the morning to see what the day brings.

- Caffeine, I recently enjoyed a detailed conversation with a brain surgeon who stated that neither he or any of his colleagues choose to drink coffee or caffeine rich drinks. Enough said, I would suggest!

I started this section by stating people pay small fortunes in order to self-inflict pollution; of course, they pay in far more important, life changing ways, than only spending a little cash. What is the point in thinking big and living success if we are too unhealthy or unfit to see it through?

19

EXERCISE IS VITAL FOR SUCCESS

Far from only taking exercise. Oh, such more than ever only taking exercise. Inspirational. On every level.

Why exactly is exercise vital for success?

With good reason!

It cannot be emphasised enough how important it is to be happy and healthy in parallel to creating your ideal financial life. You are clearly going to want to be around to enjoy the fruits of your labours and be fit enough to see your plans through to completion.

Comfort zones will be left behind and for sure there will be days when stress makes itself known...the healthier you are, the easier you will find yourself able to cope and ideally then enjoy the ride!

Practically all of my fellow coaches take regular exercise, they are convinced this a major contributor to their effectiveness and the longevity of some of their careers. There are indeed several high-profile life coaches, who although well into their seventies and some even their eighties, still regularly conduct seminars and write relevant new books.

BODY BREAKDOWN REVERSAL

As our body matures it is usual for it to start losing muscle mass, to be replaced with fat or muscle wastage, resulting in less physical strength and suppleness.

It doesn't have to be this way, not at all.

The only reason for this loss of muscle mass is due to a lack of aerobic and anaerobic exercise or put another way - our brain receives the message that we are not using our muscles in the way we once did and concludes we must no longer require them. Kick-starting the beginning of the transformational changes in our bodies commonly held to be signs of old age.

Yet paradoxically there are many examples of lean and mean octogenarians who are hugely fit and leading the kind of active lives that would put many of their grandchildren to shame.

What is the difference here, what can possibly be their miraculous secret?

In virtually all the cases these individuals have always led active lives and saw no reason to slow down or stop doing what they have always done simply because another birthday passed on by. In other words, they have kept a good high percentage of their muscle mass throughout their life.

NEVER NEED TO DIET

It seems every week a new miracle diet hits the headlines, with the usual promise of quick weight-loss by buying-into their selected new eating regime.

I have weighed the same for the past three decades. This isn't because I might not be inclined to put weight on, it is all down to eating sensibly with an eye to my long term wellbeing. While making sure my lifestyle includes plenty of aerobic exercise for fitness and some anaerobic exercise for muscle mass.

Rather than buying into yo-yo dieting, complete lifestyles for holistic wellbeing give us the best chance of maintaining our perfect weight long term.

Mindset combined with lifestyle is vital for genuine permanent weight loss. If you or I are spending every day desperately focusing on the need to lose weight and frequently glancing in the mirror online underlines this, for sure we need to adjust our mindset and then watch the difference this makes.

If all we constantly focus on is losing weight, we will constantly have weight to lose – adopting a new mindset will prove significantly more effective and work more permanently than any diet.

We instead need to focus our attention on building our lifestyle around actively becoming our vision of how we see our ideal physical self.

Cut out of this self-empowered lifestyle anything at all which is incongruous with how our vision of this ideal self looks. Instead we need to focus all of our attention on those things (healthy food/drink, regular exercise) which integrated into our lives bring this vision of our ideal physical self so much easier into genuinely being our long-term reality.

GETTING OUT WHAT YOU PUT IN

Exercise is vitally important for maintaining a healthy body and strengthening the immune system's ability to fend off disease and decay. As I mentioned earlier, our body is the vehicle used to travel around and experience all the wonders of this magnificent planet we live upon.

Investing in ourselves in terms of eating healthily and partaking of regular exercise is going to be more than worth the investment far later down our timeline when we can still run up the stairs and experience life to the full.

If you are already pretty fit keep on doing what you do and never be tempted to slacken off just because of another birthday passing by. I have always taken exercise in one form or another. I work every day at maintaining my body through sensibly eating combined with plenty of exercise. And you can do precisely the same!

I spent my time in gyms back in the day and for sure they can be an excellent starting place when venturing into getting fit for perhaps the first time in years. They will have qualified instructors to advise you on taking those first steps. It is vitally important to start gently at first. If you realistically know you are extremely unfit it is definitely wise to consult a health professional before beginning to make changes.

Regular gentle exercise is always better than nothing at all and you can always step it up once you start to feel more able. Small steps towards our goals are preferable to none at all every single time!

20

OUR NATURE TO BE FOUND IN NATURE

Today I commune with nature. My forest. My seashore
None may follow.

Many of those who live in urban environments have become completely disassociated from nature. The only nature being encountered is the green blur seen from car or train windows as we rush on by.

Us humans have a deep, you could almost call it primeval, connection to nature that exists right there in our DNA. If we become too disconnected from nature we end up living a kind of zombie-like existence. Wild areas frequently regarded as somewhere to fear.

WHAT POSSIBLE RELEVENCE DOES THIS ALL HAVE TO HAPPINESS AND ACHIEVEMENT?

Plenty!

Living 24/7 in completely artificial environments stifles creativity and deadens our intuition.

Then the need, if nature is encountered, to take some of this artificial comfort zone out there as well…

I have personally witnessed people walking deep within an ancient tranquil forest, climbing high upon a mountain or even canoeing down a river, all the while plugged into music through their headphones. Surely part of the point of being there in a forest, on a mountain or indeed in a river, is to experience the sounds as well as the sights? Isn't it rather like going to a gig by your favourite band or a classical music concert wearing a motorbike crash helmet; whatever happens, for sure you are only going to get half of the experience!

Maybe I am the one missing out here by not taking my music collection with me for a walk, yet I somehow doubt it.

TAKE A LOOK AGAIN

If you live in an urban environment, allow me to make this suggestion and I ask you to at least give it a go.

If you are one of those people who doesn't usually have the time for nature or perhaps even finds the prospect of exploring wilderness areas scary; how about you take only half an hour a couple of times a week to visit your local park? Simply sit and observe. Leave aside the headphones and no cheating yourself out of the experience by talking or texting on the phone!

Look at the trees, the grass and then listen. Hear birdsong? Do the trees make a noise? Rustling poplars or creaking old oaks. Breathe in the scents. How are they different since last time you visited? Soak up the sights, sounds and smells, feel on every level what it is like to be there.

Slowly, but absolutely surely, your connection to nature will grow stronger and you will find yourself looking forward to these visits to the park. At some point maybe venturing a little further outside your town or city to explore some more untamed nature.

OR THEN AGAIN…

Perhaps you are already very connected to nature and can't relate in any way to this section so far, living as you do in the country or on the edge of an area of wilderness?

Oh, you can help so many people!

Invite your town or city family and friends to come over to stay with you, as often as possible. Show them your reality and allow them to learn to appreciate the joy of nature through your eyes. Be their guide and show them how beautiful nature is in all her manifestations.

Exercise in nature is my first choice every time. Walking, running or tai chi within a natural setting is far from only taking exercise – it is wonderfully inspirational. Some of my best ideas have popped into my head way out in the wilderness or in the middle of a deserted ancient Neolithic site; and very rarely in the middle of a busy city!

21

THE AGGRESSIVE PATH TO NOWHERE

Loudly to make us see their point of view
Failing to listen, through their hullabaloo.

We have all met those individuals who evidently expend much of their energy aggressively attempting to convince others that they are the best at what they do or theirs is the only valid opinion worth taking on board.

If someone is the best in their field or their opinion is invariably the one to listen to, clearly this is going to be self-evident and does not require constant self-validation to others. Those who loudly proclaim to be the greatest are heading for a fall, might take a while, sure it happens every time though and the reason is clear. Constant self-validation arises from subconscious issues relating to poor confidence and inner disharmony.

If you are one who knows you self-validate please read on, this book will help you reach inner balance via overcoming self-limitation or if you know someone else who does this, then at least you can now understand it all stems from insecurity and perhaps cut them a little slack. We all have the right to grow at our own pace, as this chapter will illustrate.

The truly empowered are confident in their abilities. They play to their strengths and structure their life around how best to utilize those skills they know they possess. Rather than arrogant self-validation, they let all their actions speak for themselves and others can draw their own conclusions accordingly.

HUMILITY IS EMPOWERED

Let me define humility in the context described for our purposes – allowing others the right to have their opinion and naturally expecting the same courtesy in return. If we are proven to be right then avoiding gloating, if necessary explaining how we came to the correct conclusion and staying on good terms with those who on this occasion turned out to be incorrect.

POLITENESS COSTS NOTHING

Although bizarrely some people seem to feel that allowing consideration for others is to be showing some kind of weakness. Nothing could be further from the truth…

The stronger among us, in other words the more at peace within themselves to be personally empowered, always strive to help others and the simple act of showing appreciation with a smile can often mean so much to the recipient.

Giving of ourselves, even if this perhaps only takes the form of listening to a lonely friend or even a stranger we happened upon, for a short while, rather than constantly being the one doing the talking, transforms lives. And for sure ours!

If you or I can go through life acting with due consideration for the feelings of others we need to realise, consequently, with absolute certainty we are not always going to get things done our own way.

Yet this is okay and quite cool if you consider it as an opportunity…

Through a little compromise we can end up taking a direction we would have never even considered venturing into otherwise. Leading forward into brilliant new adventures or discovering something completely different and exciting.

The skill and art are knowing when the right moment is to assertively stick to our point of view and ensure our way is the way things happen; and when we need to back-off and go with the flow, interestingly seeing where the situation might ultimately take us.

A trend started in the West in the 1980's and in certain echelons of society has continued to grow. Politeness when dealing with others became unfashionable as the reality to some people. The hard-hitting go-getting approach seemed to have much appeal to many. As one who lived through the 1980's, I am able to observe exactly where many of these ruthlessly single-minded individuals are today and remarkably few of them seem to be living exactly what could be described as happy lives. For sure, their selfish approach to life more than likely ensured much material wealth came their way, yet money only counts for a small percentage of what it means to be entirely successful.

Without joy in the soul all the money in the world is surely not going to mean a great deal of anything much. Aggressively pursuing wealth for purely the sake of wealth is a hollow victory.

It is entirely possible to attain great wealth, by actively pursuing our dreams; the difference in the motivation is that it's the dream which is passionately attained; and the financial rewards happen as a happy secondary by-product.

WITH EXPERIENCE SOMETIMES COMES WISDOM

I confess I was once somewhat of an over-confident young man, naively thinking at well under twenty years old for sure I had this concept of life understood and how to get everything done the way I resolutely believed was the right way; which was of course according to how I saw things!

As I have already alluded to, with my million pound results, I was also something of a high flyer and doubtless more than a little precocious with it. This did not exactly always make me endearingly popular with some of my far more senior colleagues. I thought my co-workers would respect me for knowing my own mind and the frequent single-minded zealousness with which I voiced my opinions. They might have done, yet I found this wasn't how things usually played out. My results kept me in employment, not really my people skills at that point in my development!

At this stage I knew precious little about human nature and how to co-exist in harmony with others. What I didn't comprehend at that earlier point in my life is that we don't necessarily have to be greatest friends with all the people we work with or indeed even agree with everything they say. What we absolutely do need to have though is due respect for their right to actually possess their own viewpoint. Even if we are indeed later proved to be profoundly right in a discussion or decision made, that is the end of the matter.

THE GENTLE ART OF ASSERTIVENESS

There is an art to getting our point of view across and being heard in a polite and positive way, respecting others. Even if we absolutely know we are right with complete and utter certainty. Passion works better than aggression every time, calmly explaining our viewpoint rather than giving away our power by losing control.

Never intentionally making anyone else feel small or foolish once it is realised by others that we are after all correct in what we are talking about.

In other words, getting your point across in an assertive way, yet tempered with a little humility. To again clarify here I am talking about humility as a sense of respecting others right to be themselves and have their opinions, for better or worse.

The other approach, of course, would be to aggressively shout and wave your arms about, tell everyone and anyone who doesn't agree with you that they must be profoundly stupid and generally gain few friends in the process. Nobody likes big-headed people or has much respect for those who throw insults around like confetti.

Some of my colleagues who knew me back in my early career would have doubtless been quite happy to see the back of me and yet I clearly needed to go through the experience to reach where I am today.

We all have the right to evolve perfectly at our own pace, how else?

22

DESK-THUMPING IS SO LAST CENTURY

So many people busy talking at us
Aggressively vocalising what they discuss.

I hear horror stories at seminars and through my clients, workplace bullying is apparently alive and well. The tyrant approach is unbelievably still employed be some managers even in the 21st century!

Back in the early 1990's, Lee Fraser (my father, hence the same surname!) was one of five regional sales managers in a mid-sized media type business. Every month there would be a management meeting at head office and it was compulsory to attend.

The usual routine went something like this. The five regional managers were not allowed to drive to the meeting, they each had to travel by late evening train to be met at the station and taken to hotels. Each regional manager was given a different hotel to stay in; they all had one thing in common, no dining facilities or restaurant within easy walking distance.

Meetings started early at this company, the regional managers would be expected to be ready for picking-up at 7am to be driven straight to head-office.

Before 8am they were all seated around a conference table for their monthly meeting. Having been served their choice of hot drink at the commencement of the meeting that remained it as far as sustenance was concerned until the meeting broke at around 11am for a fifteen-minute recess. There were no vending machines or any other means of finding anything to eat or drink. The meeting reconvened and a further hot drink was served.

These were high pressure events, the managing director would shoutingly inform them that having almost met their targets he was unhappy as he must have set them far too low and proceeded to raise them higher. This unsmiling managing director hadn't been at the sharp end canvassing for customers for many years and was unrealistic about competition; he was completely out of touch with his marketplace and the regional managers all knew this. Can you imagine how much they respected his opinion?

A working lunch was served around 1pm consisting of a sandwich each. Around 4.30pm the meeting would finally close, with five hungry, dehydrated, tired managers being delivered to the railway station for their home journey.

My father lasted less than six months with this company, not surprisingly they had a high turnover of staff. I think the writing was probably on the wall when he took bottled water and a packed lunch to one of their monthly meetings!

He talked at length to one of the co-directors when he handed in his resignation and explained he thought their people management skills were out of the stone-age. In all fairness, the guy had to agree, he said something along the lines of the managing director feeling that keeping his managers hungry (literally apparently!) and creating the environment they were never quite sure if they would have a job from month to month would keep them on their toes and ensure they gave their most to the company cause.

Well, I suppose it's a point of view, yet not a terribly effective one.

IN THIS TOGETHER

As any empowered manager will confirm, getting the best from others requires encouragement, setting realistic targets with clear incentives once they are reached. Making staff feel part of a team and for sure here we are all working towards the same cause. Trusting them with responsibility and giving them the space to get on with their tasks (but also being available if they need help). Ensuring everyone feels comfortable within their environment, so work becomes a mutually pleasurable experience for all.

At some point, of course, someone is going to make an error - a member of staff will forget to do something, inadvertently make a poor deal or any of the other hundred and one crisis moments which happen in the day to day running of a business.

Having an open-door policy for staff to bring their issues to the manager is essential; our manager needs to be accessible to his or her co-workers. If the error isn't down to dishonesty or downright incompetence, supporting the member of staff and helping them to sort out their mess will ensure their loyalty far more than any metaphorical dragging them over hot coals. They will usually be fully aware they goofed-up and allowing them the chance to atone and make things good **team-builds brilliantly!**

As a business owner, if one of your senior managers makes an error in judgement, the automatic response for many seems to be to let them go and replace them. Far better again, unless the error is down to dishonesty or catastrophic incompetence, back them and allow them to sort their mess out. Everyone goofs-up sometimes…if it can be fixed then support the process and if it is truly beyond repair, be honest within the company and then fire-fight to recover any public loss of reputation.

MAKE IT FUN

The wise people down through the ages have always had a degree of humility and assuredly a sense of humour within their personality, plus a driven assertiveness to see through what they believe to be the right course of action.

It has been said that a sense of humour is part of the sixth sense. Laughter is contagious and mutually good medicine.

Think of all the long-term successful people, be they business entrepreneurs, humanitarians, pioneers in medicine, great athletes, entertainers or writers; most of the ones who have made their mark going on to become almost legendary, they all have certain things in common. They are passionately driven, rarely ego-centric and can often laugh at a situation or better still themselves.

A combination of assertiveness tempered with a little humility and added into the mix an enthusiastic sense of humour, will take us far in life.

23

DISCOVERING YOUR TALENTS

Got to make all those dreams come true
Take action, do it now, it's down to you.

We have all had those moments, especially in childhood playing or daydreams, where we can visualize ourselves doing a certain job. How many of us ended up following those daydreams, becoming what our subconscious was telling us?

I had dreams, I saw myself as a writer or perhaps a performer on stage of some kind. Happily, my career eventually enabled me to work within both of my dreams, as I travel to give radio, television interviews or live talks in my seminars I am performing as much as I could have ever wished to.

You see the thing is if the dream is in any way possible to literally happen for you...to become reality...then it can.

By this I mean we might dream of saving lives, which is entirely possible within an incredible variety of different choices of career; or perhaps we alternatively dream of piloting the first intergalactic space shuttle which might appear realistically impossible - unless we make it our reality by becoming an actor...there is always a way!

If the dream is literally possible, you know you really can literally make it your reality!

WHAT ARE YOU TRULY AWFUL AT?

What separates those stand-out high-achievers in any walk of life from the rest of the populous is not that they are amazingly luckier or indeed extra talented; these people have recognised what they excel at and gone right ahead to mine-it.

More importantly they are also fully aware of areas where they lack talent and wisely chose to instead work within what they can do, rather than focusing on those areas outside of their skill-set.

I know I am an entertaining communicator of concepts and ideas, I have the validation from my audiences and clients as proof of this over the course of several decades, right back to the start of my career. I also know I am able to write in an engaging way which ultimately helps others to grow, my book sales and reviews validate this.

On the other hand, I know admin tasks and small-talk are areas I lack any great skills in. I mean there are many other things I can't do such as play professional soccer, write computer programmes or dance in a way which doesn't look comical!

The point is I concentrate on those things I know that I can do, and this provides me with all the ingredients I require to succeed.

You can do exactly the same and become successful in a way you never imagined!

You are going to need a good old-fashioned journalist's notebook and a pen. Please do use this method rather than being tempted to type on your computer or phone. There is a good reason for asking you to do it this way, as information is easier to retain if physically written down rather than typed.

If you are one of those fortunate individuals who are completely content with how you earn you daily bread and would have no wish to change a thing, I am delighted for you and see you again soon in the next chapter. You know what though, alternatively you may as well stay around to read on anyway, who knows you might be able to help a friend or family member find their role in life; and then again you might just find some outrageously cool new direction within your own life!

So, maybe you never really gave much thought about how your ideal career looks? Perhaps school wasn't your ideal environment and you were pleased to finally get out of the place into the world of any kind of work?

Did your career path happen out of a desire for a safe option or was it because you were keeping alive a family tradition within a certain career choice? Maybe you are working in a job solely because parents or careers advisors at school thought it would fit you?

Or are you one of those individuals who enjoys being within academia, yet realises it is fast becoming time to spread your wings, getting out there into your possible workplace?

If you fit any category above or indeed even if you don't, yet lack direction, how about finding a career path to truly satisfy you? One you are delighted to pursue, making you look forward to each new day.

Sound good? Let's do this!

NOTEBOOK AND PEN TIME

Find a place where you are unlikely to be disturbed and start to write a list.

This list is going to consist of all the things you know for sure are **outside of your own personal skill-set**. Be careful here as it can be tempting to use this list as an excuse to stay within a comfort zone (trap).

No, on the contrary this list is about those things which, no matter if you went to University for millennia, you would still never be able to master. It is all about getting to know yourself better and the easiest way to concentrate energy into those things **we can do**, is to firstly know exactly what we can't!

To give an example I will list a few of those things outside of my own skill set:

1. Trivial small-talk, such as about the weather or how well (or not) a sports team might currently

be doing, leaves me looking blankly at the other person.

2. The finer details of business administration bore me enough to take a short nap.

3. Having any kind of empathy for lazy people or excuse makers eludes me.

4. Buying into the routine of doing the same thing day in and day out makes me quickly lose interest.

5. Turning down public speaking opportunities, even if they are apparently logistically impossible!

There are obviously more things I cannot do, and your list will more than likely look completely different.

Don't be too hard on yourself and if you feel inclined perhaps inject a little humour into your answers, but for sure be honest. There is every reason to take time over this process, as it will be helping YOU first and foremost.

NEXT

When you are done, it is time to write a fresh list on a new page.

This time I want you to write **down all those talents you know you do possess.** This isn't a time for modesty, allow yourself to get really carried away in this exercise.

Don't think rationally too much here, just let yourself automatically write.

Some of your qualities or personal skill-set might be:

1. Patience.
2. A sense of humour.
3. Kindness and/or empathy.
4. Great degrees of concentration.
5. Creativity.
6. Excellent ability in communication
7. Motivating others.
8. Compelling writing.
9. Practicality.
10. Logical thinking.
11. Studious.
12. Understanding numbers.
13. Or indeed any of the many other things you feel go together to make up the essence of who you are.

Take a little time to study your two lists.

Then more or less put out of your mind the first skill-lacking list. It is vital to go through the process of writing it, to understand yourself more clearly. Now it has done its job - it ceases to be relevant to your immediate future (keep it though, as we will briefly revisit it later to help you progress a little further down your personal path).

The important list for now is the one which details your own personal skill sets. This is the one to focus on, you see **life is about to get a whole lot more interesting!**

Back to your notepad and now write another list.

This list consists of all those things you personally enjoy doing – can be absolutely anything at all:

1. Playing a sport.
2. Reading.
3. Crosswords.
4. Talking.
5. Martial arts.
6. Knitting.
7. Driving and/or travelling.
8. Painting.
9. Singing in the shower.
10. Politics.
11. Gardening.
12. Poetry.

13. Woodworking.

14. Chess.

15. Flying kites.

16. Or any of the million and one other things (however abstract) you might derive pleasure from practising.

NOW WE NEED TO NARROW THINGS DOWN A LITTLE

Take some time to cross out all those things on your skill-set list which do not represent the very essence of who you know you are.

Leave yourself only three entries, which are those top three things you know are positively powerfully true to you.

Your personal enjoyment list comes next. Again, cross out any secondary interests, leaving only the top three things you know for sure you consistently love to do.

So now you will have two lists (plus the one we are ignoring for now) along with a bit of a mess made with all those crossings-out!

Take a fresh page and write the three remaining entries from each list in two parallel lines across the top of the page.

Which might read something like this…

Personal Skills: Communication, Writing, Studious
Favourite things to do: Walking in Nature, Talking Politics, Making Clothes

---

Underneath those lines make a brand-new list of any possible careers which can combine at least one of your favourite ways to spend your time, with a matching personal skill.

- An example would be the person who loves walking in nature and has amazing communication skills – possible careers beckon as a national park ranger or tourist guide taking people out into wild areas.
- Another example is the individual spending every spare moment thinking about or discussing politics and who happens to be skilled in writing – a career starting out with political journalism leading to brilliant personal satisfaction from

covering elections and interviewing politicians; or maybe embarking upon a political career themselves at some point down the line.

- To finish, one final example is the person who has always made their own much-admired clothes and is studious – they might want to go study fashion at Uni or College, get that fashion design degree and make a career out of their hobby.

FORGET ABOUT BACK-UP PLANS

You don't need a back-up plan, just commitment and persistence…

I had been just as willing to buy into this one as most of us are. This is one major learning opportunity for all of us and definitely transformed my life once I opted out of this mindset of limitation.

We come up with a brilliant, inspirational idea – one we can buy-into on every level and immediately start looking for ways to make it happen, for it to manifest for real in our life.

Yet, at the back of our mind we think "yeah, but what will I do if this doesn't work out?"

So, we come up with a back-up plan for if it all fails.

If our goals are worth committing to, they deserve our 100% commitment. You and I do ourselves a massive disservice if at the back of our minds all the while we are thinking "well, you know, if this doesn't work out, I'll just go with whatever else" This mindset sets us up for failure every time!

Forget about back-up plans...mindfully commit to exactly what you are pursuing right now and focus all of your attention on making it work for you.

Leave yourself with no choice but to commit...and then whatever occurs to impede your progress (it's how we learn and grow) you are going to find a way around, over or under that hurdle. We can only develop this success centred mindset by forgetting about potential failure to kick-out forever that back-up plan!

Being adaptable within whatever we are heading, as we are on this journey is essential...to ensure we get wherever we want to utilize all feedback as our own satellite navigation...constantly refining and adjusting our course until we arrive at our destination.

That is why it is vitally important, before even beginning our journey to at least have some idea of where we are actually heading!

Those routes to getting there play out and evolve as we travel towards dreams, which is a different matter altogether and the exiting bit actually of this journey we have chosen.

In the meantime, it's extremely useful to keep at the forefront of your mind when thinking about the future you are shaping for yourself this or something even better! Then your plans can evolve to grab any unexpected new opportunities which present themselves.

24

BE A HELICOPTER PILOT!

Your perfect vision of your own life
as you always dreamed it can be.

An airplane needs a lengthy runway to take off. Our helicopter can take off vertically, just as we can when we say YES to those often unexpected opportunities which come along which take us straight up to a totally new level of success.

The airplane needs half the sky to change direction. Our helicopter can change direction instantly, just as we can continually adapt to whichever direction our intuition is telling us we need to go next.

This airplane again requires a long runway to land. Our helicopter can hover and land anywhere which seems interesting, just as it is valuable for us to stop occasionally to see the bigger picture, which might lead to us choosing to touch base with new experiences.

So be a helicopter pilot!

YOU ONLY NEED TO SEE THE NEXT STEP

Attempt to logically work out how to get from the point you are at now - to where you desire to be, and you miss out on all the fun!

I mentioned earlier in the book life is all about the journey...being completely open to any opportunities which come our way and being ready to go with our gut feeling or intuition to see where saying YES takes us.

Rationally second-guessing the whole road to our destination is an utterly self-defeating exercise. Knowing where we want to arrive clearly matters a lot – the wonderful unpredictability of whatever will unfold before us getting there and recognising these opportunities through using our intuition is for sure the ridiculously exciting bit!

My first business venture for myself was a wholesale company selling to the alternative gift industry across the UK, some other areas of Europe and Canada. What became apparent over the course of running the business for a while is no trade magazine for our industry existed. With my background in publishing I said YES to creating just such a magazine to help gift shops find myself and fellow wholesalers. Producing and editing the magazine put me in touch with several exiting new trade contacts, which helped my wholesale business to thrive even more. Eventually as the internet started to become most gift shops primary resource, I stopped producing the magazine, but didn't take the obvious step of going online with it. I believe we need to follow our passions, running an online directory failed to ignite much interest in me. What did happen as a result of my time spent running my own publishing house, alongside the wholesale business, is it placed me in direct touch with countless high-level media contacts. When I eventually turned full time with writing and life coaching there I already had a ready-placed arena to raise my profile (usually for free) and this quickly grabbed the attention of the very people I might help.

Did I plan all of this our beforehand? How could I foresee when I started my wholesale company that I would end up writing articles for magazines all across the world to help so many people change their lives for the better?

I have the habit of simply saying YES if it feels right, this has taken me far and it will do the same for YOU as well!

This is what led to me running a lucrative car-washing business at fourteen years old. A neighbour suffered from a migraine, with her dirty car parked on the driveway and me taking pity on her discomfort I offered to wash it for her. This resulted in half the rest of the neighbourhood relying upon my services to keep their vehicles clean each week. Again, had I planned this beforehand? Nope, I was only being neighbourly to help someone out; and yet found myself quite happy to say YES to all the other neighbours who liked the job I had done, and all the extra cash proved pretty handy as well!

Having a clear concept of where we are heading is vital, our inner vision of how our life looks in terms of when we get there needs to be treasured.

What also needs to be treasured are those opportunities which for sure will come our way on the journey. You or I never need to know before how every single step will play-out on the way, we do need to be flexible enough to adapt and just be ready to say YES when the time for action arrives. As it always does.

One more seriously bizarre example from my own life we briefly visited a little earlier in Alive to Thrive when we talked about comfort traps, also perfectly illustrates how saying YES to a totally leftfield offer can take us somewhere we would have surely never even contemplated before!

I had written poetry for years and enjoyed going to listen to hear performance poets live. Having taken myself off to see a local poetry collective do their thing I admit it did cross my mind it seemed quite fun to be up there sharing poetic tales. Talking to the organiser after to congratulate him on the awesome show, I found I already knew him through his having attended one of my life coaching events. He asked if I might like to perform at his next poetry event in a few weeks and I instantly replied YES.

Performing poetry opened a whole new area of creativity for me, leading to going on a few solo UK tours as a poet; and some outrageously unprecedented exposure through taking part in many radio interviews and tv appearances to talk poetry. Which led to me being offered and saying YES to my own arts radio show. Which moved on to now having my own in-house recording studio to produce my syndicated Beyond Poetry Radio Show, growing to be heard via multiple community radio stations by over a quarter million listeners around the world each week. The other beauty about having a recording studio is I can also produce my own audio books, be those coaching centred or indeed poetry. My audio books allow me to practically reach millions of people worldwide, many of whom would never otherwise have the chance to hear some of the essence of what I impart during one of my seminars.

Did I plan any of this beforehand? Absolutely not!!! I have always been ready for the chance to say YES and see where it might take me though.

It never ceases to astound me how one door opening before us and saying YES, can take us off on the most fascinating and outrageously wonderful journey we might never have imagined in our wildest dreams.

And you or I would miss out on all of this if we rigidly stuck to the way we had planned it all out before.

We need to be open to opportunities and flexible enough to take necessary action when we spot them. Learning to trust in our intuition, rather than attempting to logically pre-plan, is one of the most vital skills needed to live on our terms and most of all, have some fun along the way!

DO PLAN THIS THOUGH

It can be all too easy to find reasons to talk ourselves out of the life we deserve. Planning for sure does come in useful here in terms of getting started and keeping up the momentum.

So, what does your ideal lifestyle look like? What did you identify as your perfect career choice? Think it might be impossible to get there? Think again!

- Does it require qualifications you don't already have? You won't have the time to study? Take evening classes at a local College or University, if that is not practical opt to enrol for an online qualification that need only take a few hours a week out of your time. You might have to re-arrange your schedule to fit all the study in, in all honesty so what? I am sure you will agree it is worth the effort when for all the long-term brilliance it will bring to your life.

- Is experience needed? Ask if it is possible to observe or work in a voluntary unpaid capacity part-time in to gain experience. A friend of mine did this at a whole-food café and gained a wealth of experience in the functioning of such a type of business. Now he is well on his way to starting his own similar enterprise in another town.

It is possible to come up with a thousand and one excuses to not make that first move. You know what? The time is never right if you think it isn't! The perfect time to start is always right now…you don't need anything but the self-discipline and desire to keep on keeping on.

I promise you that when you do take some action and start to see the progress you are making to get to where you ought to be, the feeling is incomparable.

Take that first step now. Remember you really don't need to know where the next step is, it will become crystal clear where and when the time has arrived to move things forward on to that second and then third step.

25

SEE WHAT YOU HAVE ALREADY GOT

The true path is still to look deep within.
All answers already known.

The very career you would be thrilled to be engaged in right now might be hiding in plain sight!

This takes the skill-set exercise we undertook a couple of chapters ago a little bit further out there somewhere! Take a few moments to allow yourself another sidelong glance at what you love to do and see if a possible career lays there waiting, one which you might never have noticed before.

This story perfectly illustrates the point. Pete spent all his spare time engrossed in photography. He worked in sales, he was good as well and usually topped the monthly charts at the company he worked for. It never

213

really crossed his mind to do anything other than sales, after all it paid for his quite rich lifestyle. He came to my attention after the company he worked for ceased to exist, having been bought out by a mega-corporation with their own established sales team, Pete found himself unexpectedly made redundant. Although he might easily apply for and get another sales job, this abrupt interruption to his well established routine served as a clarion wake-up call; and as he was now already in his mid-thirties, inevitably he wondered where he might be career wise when he hit forty.

Whichever way he considered his future, sales was definitely not the job he wanted to be doing for the rest of his working life. We looked around at other possible options for him. Asking him his favourite way to spend his down-time, he replied playing tennis and photography. And Pete then continuously enthused for well over fifteen minutes (barely pausing for breath!) about some of his photographs having already been published in several glossy magazines. These lightbulb moments really do happen sometimes! We looked at one another and Pete burst-out laughing. Right there, hiding in plain sight, was his future career. He already had a great portfolio of some high-end published work, with his sales-drive all he needed to do was search through the many thousands of photographs in his archive matching them up to suitable potential magazines and go right ahead to pitch to get them in there. Did he make it a success? You bet he did and more importantly Pete tells me he is happier than at any other time in his life; and still enjoys his rich lifestyle.

During my sabbatical for a year through 2015 I wrote the original transcript of this book but reclusively did not commit to any live coaching shows or promote myself as open for business.

The question became when returning to full fitness became how to re-establish myself? The business world changes incredibly quickly and taking myself out of the game for a year inevitably I found myself also out of the loop commercially.

Without planning it all out too much I did have an intuitive sense of how to not only get myself once more out in front of people, I had the feeling I might actually be able to do this in a way where my profile would be raised far beyond anything I had ever considered possible before.

This time round I knew I wanted to reach out to help people all around the world…

Firstly, I set up an events, publishing and admin company www.deanfrasercentral.com to handle the day to day running of my diary to ensure I honoured all my commitments.

Then I used all of my three decades of communication experience to get commissions writing self-help articles for numerous magazines truly right across the globe, while enjoying the by-product of the outrageous level of publicity this generated!

I gave interviews in whatever media, whenever they were requested; and also sent paper and digital copies of the my other books all over the world to be reviewed.

Giving myself the target of reaching at least five new contacts every single day and by working diligently for over a year, I got there. I became an "overnight" success story, through trusting my message would step-up to work on a global scale. I happily found my opinion also now sought at a spectacularly higher level than I ever enjoyed prior to my self-healing year.

Each year since I easily reach in excess of fifteen million people through my books, audios, live shows, radio and above all my columns for magazines. Had I not experienced the health challenge, I am sure I would never have seen the bigger picture and enthusiastically gone for this global presence. And yet this option was there all the time, hiding in plain sight.

> **What skills do you already have? Are you in possession of something which perhaps only requires a little lateral thought and the right marketing to give you everything you might wish for?**

THE RIGHT KIND OF EDUCATION

Say you adore cooking and are already a brilliant cook, everyone loves your meals and it is an established fact beyond any possible doubt. Your dream might be quite naturally to work within your labour of love and open a restaurant.

What steps to take next? The conventionally accepted route would take you off to catering college for several years to achieve a degree, to subsequently possess a certificate showing that you can cook. Yet that is already an established fact, so would it not be rather a waste of your energy, valuable time and more than likely a considerable quantity of cash?

A far more useful course of action would be to take a shorter, comprehensive business management degree and a food hygiene course. A ridiculously high percentage of restaurants fail within their first year and this usually has practically nothing to do with the quality of their cuisine. It's about marketing, sourcing raw ingredients at the lowest prices and the bottom line or in other words making that all important profit! You are going to be different though, as you have studied business management you will be fully equipped to ensure right from day one that your restaurant is built upon solid foundations.

Looking for investors suddenly became way easier, with your business management degree you know exactly how to pitch and get their serious attention – and investment capital.

How many of us genuinely work within exactly the qualifications we achieved, I certainly never have and although body language has proved invaluable in my life, the kind of career choices open to me as solely a body language psychologist held little appeal. I will nevertheless share a few body language tips starting on page 255 of the book. For now…

The other point to bear in mind here is a dramatically high number of those high achievers, I mean the mega successful entrepreneurs, either dropped out of college or never went there in the first place. Their constant drive, enthusiasm and passion for the negotiating process and seeing through their deals, brings them amazing financial rewards. Yet for many of these tycoons, mega amounts of hard currency are only the happy by product of working every day within a process they passionately love.

Far from being in any way down on education, what I am suggesting here instead is a kind of flexible lateral thinking. Of course, if you wish to be a doctor, lawyer, scientist or any of the other professions requiring dedicated study you need to go ahead to excel within education, earn your degree with first class honours and follow that dream all the way to its brilliant conclusion of working within your chosen career.

On the other hand, perhaps we might already possess a talent hiding in plain sight talent? And to work in a career utilizing that talent does not absolutely require a certificate from a college to say we can. Like Pete earlier, all we might need instead is that talent and some passion to make our own dream happen. As Pete himself says, "not one of the magazines my photographs appear in has ever questioned what kind of qualifications I possess to be a photographer" they instead prefer to pay him great fees to utilize his natural talents!

If we do choose to further educate ourselves is it not it wiser to instead go down the route of adding to our skill-set with something to assist in making our dream a successful long-term reality?

IS THERE A JOB AT THE END OF IT?

If taking the steps to further educate ourselves, we need to be sure there is a potential career we would love to be involved with waiting at the end of our degree.

Lisa spent three years studying philosophy, and a further two years getting her masters. I met her when I took my car in for routine servicing and she was working on reception at the garage. Do be sure when making the commitment to several years' worth of study there are career options waiting at the end. Lisa is now looking for positions as a lecturer in philosophy, having realised her choice of study, while it certainly fascinated her during the process, left her with a narrowly limited number of career avenues open for potential employment.

INSTANT GRATIFICATION

The information technology driven world in which we exist results in us possessing the answer to virtually any question or the background to an individual we want to know more about, right there at our fingertips.

This can lead many of us to expect similar kinds of instant results from our lives. **Life rarely works this way.** For sure we can find ourselves in brilliant new adventures by developing the habit of saying YES to those leftfield opportunities. The building of a completely new lifestyle though takes dedication and persistence.

This is exactly why so many of the that-doesn't-work-on-to-the-next readers of books such as Alive to Thrive (those loosely labelled as self-help titles) fail to follow through on their ideas and dreams. These people are often tantalizingly close to their wildest dreams transforming their lives, but as it does take time and effort, they quit. And it might have all played out so differently.

Expectation is clearly vital to change anything at all. Dramatic new lifestyles require equally dramatic new mindsets from us.

Building a house first requires firm foundations, it is precisely the same with building a future full of outrageously new big ideals. Only once the foundations are in place, in our case this would be having established what we genuinely want from life or indeed our lifestyle, then the real construction proceeds. Then we can go right ahead to see where this journey will take us and that is when the fun begins!

If we have always consistently done things one way and then suddenly change our focus this will take a while to show-up in our life. It is just how it works. To overcome often years of poor thinking does require a concerted, long-term effort on our part and the resultant Energy shift then gradually sees the transformation start in our daily life.

Think of it like going off to university, here though the lecture hall is your own life.

You wouldn't expect to qualify as a doctor in three months, becoming proficient at taking control of your own life is exactly the same. Mastery comes with experience. Learning opportunities will be encountered. You are educating yourself and your ongoing life is the lecturer.

Every time we overcome some deeply entrenched mindset which might have somehow limited our ideal lifestyle from existing, we are placing ourselves so much closer to its permanence.

MAKING IT LAST

If we love the thought of wearing a designer suit each day, but our success mindset is incongruent with this reality, we will never feel at ease within that lifestyle. It will feel odd or like we are playing dress-up!

Re-read this book until you feel able to let-go of anything at all which might hold you back within your thoughts or mindsets. Living rich is never only about our bank balance, it is crucially feeling comfortable within success and whatever that personally means to us.

26

THE HELP IS OUT THERE

Network with the more experienced.
Knock on all those doors.

You would be surprised at how usefully helpful established, successful people can be if you simply ask them. They usually enjoy sharing their experiences and stories about how they got to where they are.

Cultivate the habit of asking those who have already been there and done that. The internet makes this considerably easier, most of us having some type of online presence. Those who are already walking their talk within the area we wish to venture are often directly contactable by email or social networking sites.

Ask nicely and the likelihood is you are going to get a reply. We don't need to travel our path alone. There is a wealth of talented assistance available to help us on our way.

Prove this one for yourself by emailing someone you admire within whatever field interests you and ask a question – unless they are unbelievably ignorant (and frankly why would want to email such a person anyway?!) chances are you will get a reply.

I have done this type of networking many times over the years and built up an extended network of magically talented people from all areas of success, business through to the creative arts and I call upon them for opinions or advice. You can follow my example to do precisely the same. We don't necessarily have to follow their advice...but more of that shortly!

IN HARMONY

What if parts of your skill-sets aren't in harmony to your talent, as an example - you might be an amazing singer but lacking a commercial mindset haven't got a clue how to make this pay? Then it is time to form a mutually beneficial partnership with a person you trust who can help you achieve all you have the potential to bring into your life.

Another story from my archives illustrates this point perfectly, the time I freely and willingly helped a struggling artist.

Raine is the most extraordinary of artists, her style fantasy art inspired by mythology. The first time I came across her, Raine had entered an arts café where I happened to be enjoying a sage tea, to see if they might display her work to perhaps sell some. I have to say, impressed as I was by her artwork, Raine herself was not one of life's natural sales people!

As she far too modestly proceeded to sell herself short and dramatically undervalue her vivid art, I seriously had to restrain myself from jumping in to stop her from talking. Instead I gave her my card and suggested I might be able to help. Thankfully she contacted me. Putting her in touch with some prestige art galleries took her work into an entirely different arena, they loved her art as much as I did and remarkably soon she found herself making a great living from her creative endeavours. Her new found confidence, after proprietors of high-end galleries validated she paints beautifully, enables her to ask quite literally ten times the price from where she previously valued her art.

There is always a way and if you do personally lack some of the skills which will enable you to fly - you need to actively seek out someone who will compliment your talents. Local networking is an excellent place to start, is there a Chamber of Trade or Commerce in your area? Or are there meeting places or clubs for those who, like yourself, are perhaps starting out in a new direction with their career or seeking to grow within their existing work choice? Skill sharing is happily growing as a phenomenon. Through networking either online or in person you can find exactly what or who you need.

WELL-MEANING ADVICE TO USUALLY IGNORE

Friends and family can for sure offer us much appreciated support within our endeavours, by believing in what we are doing and morally supporting us to help us stay on track. Uncle Bob may be a wise and wonderful guy, but if he hasn't actually done what you want to do, chances are his advice will only be well-meaning opinions with no hard facts to back them up.

Far better we seek out those high-fliers within our field of endeavour and listen to what they might have to say. Those experts who have been there, done that and can offer real practical advice to guide us.

By the way, we are never obliged to HAVE to take their advice. The more feedback we can obtain though within any potential directions to take, the easier it is to make decisions and ultimately the best way is still always opting to go with our intuition or that gut feeling!

In my own experience business advisors within banks and similar financial institutions may well be highly qualified, although crucially they have never usually physically run businesses or had any direct experience in dealing with the complexities of managing a team of employees. Do ensure to take the time to validate any advice you might get from business advisors at banks. Check it out with others who possess proven track-records with real experience of running business successes to call upon. If you can't personally network with those top-of-the-tree movers and shakers in your career choice, instead absorb their autobiographies and watch online vids or vlogs if they have one. Step into their mindset to see what they might do faced with your choice.

The same goes for accountants, their financial advice may well be spot-on, but never take for granted that it is necessarily going to be right for you.

Be sure to take the time to ponder all practical options before making a commitment to any course of action which affects the long-term viability of your business venture and then go with your gut feeling in the end. And 99.9% of the time that will be the right choice!

GO HUSTLE A LITTLE TO GET WHERE YOU WANT

Okay, I guess the word hustle does have a few negative permutations attached. Rather than suggesting you con or swindle anyone (generally resulting in the fast track to jail!) here I am using hustle in the sense of creating your own energetic opportunities to realise your dream.

It doesn't matter if you or I are looking at getting a new career or seeking to fulfil all our potential within a job we are already doing, there are ways to help ourselves keep that good energy flowing and neatly avoid The Third Thought self-talk or finding ourselves locked in a comfort trap.

Networking is a wonderful way of opening doors and easing your personal pathway to where you deserve to be.

The only way to discover answers is to ASK! When looking for information, advice or even a job...you clearly must be prepared firstly to ask the question. You have got to be prepared to go that extra mile, in fact as many miles as it takes!

By the way, I would always rather risk looking silly for a moment by asking about something I am unsure of than remain uninformed every single time! And others will respect you all the more for having the intelligence and confidence to ask - instead of witnessing you struggling to muddle through.

By asking you need to be prepared to risk being turned away. Occasionally it is going to play out that way, other times though wonderful opportunities can arise because you were prepared to metaphorically or perhaps literally knock on a few doors. Persistence always pays dividends. Nurture and develop the mindset of being doggedly determined to continually pleasantly ask for what you want and carry right on until you get the answers you seek, however long it takes...

Selling our own services or talents, we must become our very own personal publicity seeking marketing manager. I did exactly that when successfully launching forth once again after my break into the already overcrowded marketplace of life-coaching. Yet we all have that one thing to set us apart from the rest, I recognized this as my vision to help as many people as possible and the way I might do this became so obvious I wondered how I had never seen it before! And you can do precisely the same, go ahead to find that something which sets you apart within your own skill-set and talents.

What can YOU also do to give yourself some edge? Assuming it is already a given that you possess the self-belief in your new reality (dreams) manifesting for you (and if you don't, please go find a different one to completely buy-into and believe!) how can you passionately get that message across to others in a quick decisive way - meaning they will sit up and take notice of you?

If your business idea requires outside finance, ensure you come up with a realistic business plan including fantastically memorable soundbites, solid projections and scrupulously accurate figures.

Alternatively, if you wish to gain extra qualifications to help you in your dream, examine the possibility of joining a company for a while that offers on the job training while they pay for your college course; with the added benefit of getting a wage while you study

and all that extra direct experience to take forward later. Bit of a no-brainer if you think about it and if this concept can be made to fit within your projected future career. There are many such companies out there - go find them and pitch to get that job!

If your desired career involves working in the arts, teaching or helping others, look at the possibility of funding being available either locally or nationally to help you pay the costs for studying. Metaphorically open those doors for yourself and send those emails.

Opportunities are there to be taken, for sure though there are times when we need to create our own opportunities by making them happen for us.

Lateral approaches are always preferable to the route most taken. I tend to look at what everyone else is doing, their tried and often worn-out tired methods; and then do the polar opposite. How many writers see their direct role as personally becoming a publicity machine for their own work? It is generally accepted that we employ someone else to do all that for us, yet who else possibly has our own best interests most at heart and is better able to answer any potential questions, in my case about the original edition of this book!? Being right there first-hand at the coal face meant when opportunities presented themselves they were more easily able to be immediately taken.

Hustle can be a positive word...turn over every stone, send those emails, network with the more experienced, knock on all those doors, set aside plenty of seriously fun thinking-outside-the-box-time seeking those far-out methods to generate ways of getting yourself where you deserve to be as quickly as possible. Ask and then ask some more.

You will be doing yourself the greatest favour by developing the self-discipline and determination to persist until you get the results you desire.

Reticence never achieved a thing...asking always does!

QUESTIONS WE ASK OURSELVES MATTER!

The results we achieve long-term depends in the inner questions we ask ourselves when thing don't go quite according to plan or when presented with challenges in life.

If our reactions are "why do these things always happen to me?" or "don't I have enough problems already?" do you imagine we are placing ourselves in a resourceful mindset?

If we truly want to transform our lives, we had better start asking ourselves more empowering questions. "What can I learn from this situation" or "what can I do differently to avoid this happening again?"

EVERYBODY SAY YES!

I cannot repeat this too many times or emphasize it enough, when a new opportunity arrives in front of you that feels right, say YES!

Taking the steps to evolving our life inevitably leads to many incredible opportunities coming our way, with absolute certainty this will happen. It did with me and most others I know, for sure it will naturally with you as well. We need to be awake to these opportunities...

I ended up with my own radio show and residency on a TV station for a while, by saying YES to the opportunities which presented themselves.

Get into the mindset of saying YES to as many of those wonderful new experiences that come your way as possible, the ones which your intuition says go for. At least to start off with. If nothing else it will greatly aid in the leaping out of comfort traps, far more than that though this is living life large and to the full.

Comfort traps and Third Thought self-limiting inner conversations will not stand a chance if you cultivate the habit of saying YES without considering other options!

The strange thing about these new opportunities is that quite often they bizarrely happen along when we are least expecting them. Perhaps it has been an especially challenging day, or we are feeling more than a little over tired. Some happy chain of events occurs completely out of the blue and suddenly an entirely new vista opens before us. This is the time to act, especially if we are not particularly feeling in the mood…say YES and go do it anyway!

> **Opportunities are presented to be taken. It is up to us to grab them by both hands, tweak life on the nose a bit and see where the energy of saying YES can take us.**

SAY NO TO REJECTION

All throughout this book my emphasis has been on encouraging everyone to say YES to those opportunities which our intuition tells us are ones to go for.

Yet there are times when saying NO is equally strongly following our intuition. If we want to take ourselves where we deserve to be, we need to get into the habit of rejecting rejection!

Conventional wisdom for this kind of book would now have me list all types of individuals in the public eye over the last few hundred years who carried right on to the fulfilment of the dream, despite hundreds of rejections, they said NO and doggedly carried right on to make the next opportunity. You all know the stories, the author of the books about the wizard with glasses getting turned-down by publishers multiple times or the guy experimenting away to brighten our lives who eventually had his light-bulb moment. Instead I want to tell you about Lance.

Ever since Lance could remember he wanted to be a make-up artist. Making people look stunning was his passion and he would practice on various family members from quite an early age, eventually becoming quite proficient. When he left school, Lance approached all the beauty salons within twenty five miles of where he lived to ask if he might become their apprentice, while going part-time to University to study. To be turned down flat by every single one! They either didn't have any openings or felt he might not quite fit into their established team.

Lance still enrolled in University regardless of these rejections and came to my attention with only a few months of education left to the formality of getting his qualification. This is when he started to despair about ever having a career doing something he loved.

We went through a slightly different version of the Discovering Your Talents exercise, we already knew his skill set and the career he wanted to work in; but having been rejected by every beauty salon in the area, Lance sought to know how he might still make his dream happen. Starting his own business was not an option as this held little interest to him, he just wanted to be creative and get payed for being creative. We made a list of possible careers utilizing both his skills and passion. One lateral option stood out as perfect for him and this was certainly something which seriously excited him. After a little research online, Lance found, applied for and got a position working as a make-up artist on a television drama series. By saying NO to rejection Lance now works in a job he would surely do for nothing and yet actually gets well payed for instead.

When I approached magazines and e-zines after my self-imposed gap-year to write for them I got about 30% who said YES. Do you think I focused on the 70% who rejected my offer and turned me down? Not for a second! I rejected their rejection, put it out of my mind completely and got on with writing great articles for the ones who said YES. After all, for every hundred magazines I approached, I got thirty new ones to write for!

If you have some unique new niche product or service to offer, be discerning enough to say NO if a deal doesn't feel right. If you truly are innovating within a marketplace, hold out for that deal you are thrilled to say YES to instead.

Never buy into the fear of doing something different or new as an excuse to say NO. Just going to keep us in a comfort trap and as we have already established, that's seldom comfortable. Unless it feels so fundamentally wrong deep within it hurts, in which case give the offer a resounding NO.

Learn to say NO to what feel like offers too good to be true (which let's face it, they often turn out to be), those which our instinct is screaming at us to avoid like they are poison, chances that's exactly what they are!

Having a publishing company of my own, producing the trade magazine for the alternative gift industry, led to an offer coming my way. A guy I had known since my old corporate days somehow found out what I was up to over ten years down the line and got in touch with a proposition. He also had a publishing business. The deal he put on the table would see us joining forces, he would look after sales and my in-house design team would produce our publications. On the face of it a great win/win. Yet something didn't feel right. The figures all stacked-up well, but my uneasy gut feeling told me to walk away. So, I said NO. Three months later I heard through the grapevine he had gone majorly bankrupt; had I joined forces with him chances are he might well have taken me with him.

Saying NO can equally be literally to an opportunity before us which feels fundamentally wrong or instead to reject rejection to keep on keeping on.

Lance by refusing to give-up to proclaim, "I will still follow my dream!" even after all the rejections from over twenty beauty salons, now works within a career area which had never even crossed his mind.

We never need to know all the steps to where we desire to be, only hold the vision of us doing our chosen job and for sure the way will become obvious in due course.

Say YES to all those outrageously awesome new experiences, no matter if they scare us a little, all is as it needs to be.

And say NO to those things which our intuition is telling us can only lead to something which is worth actually being scared stiff at the prospect of!

27

GETTING CLOSER

Taking his leave of that place
And his former life.

There are always actions we can take to move us a step or two closer to our dreams being our life. Doesn't matter how tiny those steps are, walk enough of them and sure as anything we are going to arrive where we want to be someday. Daily action is essential to stay on track and avoiding falling into limiting mindsets or self-defeating inner conversations.

What action can you or I take every single day to move closer to our goals?

- Getting closer every day can be joining an online forum relating to our goals.

- Sending an email to someone influential - even if for the moment it is only to introduce ourselves or ask a polite question.
- Setting aside time to read something personally inspirational for an hour each day – more on just how vital this is shortly.
- Making a professional social networking page or website/blog.
- Spending enjoyable time imaging and seeing clearly our dream life.
- And prepare for success by investing in you.

Or anything else relevant to your particular dream.

READING AS AN ANCHOR

I put aside some time for reading every day, I cannot emphasise enough how this is essential! Even looking across the room in my creative space to my personal library of books I have already absorbed inspires me, happy all that knowledge is within me to call upon, as and when required.

Reading though not only adds to our knowledge, more importantly reading personally inspirational books, magazines or websites/blogs on a day to day basis reminds us of our self-set mission. Consciously and subconsciously programming ourselves with just how important this is to us.

It is all too easy to get distracted and for the mundane to take centre stage in our lives, reading is the perfect way to constantly re-adjust our radar and stay focussed.

You need to live and breathe your success mindset, reading is the anchor. You will find it considerably easier for yourself if you read personally inspirational words every day.

WRITE IT DOWN

Keep a diary or journal. A paper one. Each day write down at least five tasks (however small) for yourself to take you closer to your chosen new reality becoming your life and do them! Ticking them off as done is incredibly motivating and will keep you on track. I have done this for years and resolutely believe this simple action has helped me to reach where I am now; and will continue to enable to me to grow within my abilities to communicate to others the ways to help them personally grow.

Typically, my self-set tasks each day, listed in my own journal might read something like this:

1. Reply to any emails received in the last 24 hours.
2. Write at least one new article for a magazine.
3. Contact at least one new magazine or e-zine to ask if we might mutually benefit from combining my writing, with their core message.
4. Ensure everything is running everyone is happy at my company www.deanfrasercentral.com; then leave them to get on with what they are good at!
5. Spend some of my time daydreaming (seriously!) usually leading to fresh writing ideas or new marketplaces I might reach.

Developing a success mindset is a constant work in progress, evolving with us to take us all the way and the journey never ends, as we shall see later.

Constant vigilance is needed if we are to keep on track for where we deserve to be. Distractions and cul-de-sacs are going to be frequently encountered.

There are a few tricks you or I can utilize, enabling us to carry on moving forward. Personal mind-training exercises: buy into them, practice them often - your goals become realistic in your subconscious mind and infinitely more achievable.

Do your homework and you will keep your focus intact!

SEE IT CLEARLY

Can you imagine yourself living that ideal life? Dreams you have held for so many years, finally acted upon and coming to be your life? The utopia you always secretly thought was possible excitingly becoming your everyday reality?

It doesn't matter if rather like a game of snakes and ladders it may not always take the most direct route. It is the pictures in your own minds eye of where you will eventually be and the utter belief in the reality of your life once you are there which ensures your dreams can go all the way and you will stay on track, whatever happens.

As we saw earlier, we never need to see every step which will lead us there, planning it all out stops those leftfield opportunities from being grabbed.

Take time to fill out these fourteen questions and write the answers down in your notebook:

1. What job are you doing, and do you work every day?
2. Do you work alone or with others?
3. Who are your friends?
4. Where is your main house, what does it look like, how many rooms and how are they decorated, is there a garden, how does that look?
5. Where are your vacations and how many do you take each year?
6. Do you have a holiday home, where is it, what does that look like?
7. What's in your wardrobe and shoe closet?
8. What's your partner like, if you have one?
9. How do you spend your money?
10. Do you wear jewellery, what's it like?
11. What do you like to do in your spare time?
12. What do you eat and drink?
13. What car do you drive?
14. Literally how do you spend an entire typical day?

Think about these fourteen points often and take the time to really fill out the finer points, customize your requirements down to the smallest detail. The clearer and more refined your answers to these questions the better.

Keep all of this in mind as you fall asleep each night and you will programme yourself to accept the reality of you living this way.

28

TAKE ON THAT ROLE – PLAY THE PART

"All the world's a stage, and all the men and women merely players" William Shakespeare, the incomparable playwright summed up life quite succinctly in this quote from As You Like It.

Think back to your childhood, we all role played. Children have acting out make believe down to a fine art. If you have children of your own or perhaps know a friend who does, you will know exactly what I am talking about – when you are a child you can make believe you are pretty much anything or anyone and then act accordingly to play out that accepted role.

ADULT LIFE IS COMPLETELY THE SAME!

Take the example of Aisha training to be a lawyer. Off she goes to University for six years to fulfil her dream. How much of the process she goes through is about learning the law and how much is about taking on the mindset of being a lawyer? We expect certain standards of behaviour from our legal specialists and are more likely to commission a lawyer to work for us if they act roughly within the generally accepted parameters of a lawyer. We would probably feel far less inclined to trust our important legal matters to a lawyer dressed in ripped jeans and a heavy metal t-shirt, who calls us mate in every sentence. Aisha studies and spends her leisure time in the company of fellow law students, without consciously planning it that way, as well as learning the finer points of law she gradually takes on the mindset of being a lawyer.

We expect certain mindsets from certain professions and feel trepidation if faced with someone when their personal energy and actions don't seem to fit within accepted guidelines.

This applies to any profession or pursuit. Would we go off for a week into the wilderness with the guide who forgets our name five seconds after we have told them and fails to carry any navigation equipment? Or pay to go and see the actor who plainly hates his audience.

We can do so much to help ourselves here!

Say you want to be a writer. Do your homework. Read about fellow writers. Autobiographies, blogs, magazine articles, anything at all which aids in an understanding of what makes them tick. What is the successful writer's mindset within your chosen genre? What do they do all day? How is their schedule organized?

Good start, next think of yourself AS a writer! You are not going to be a writer perhaps one day after training - you ARE a writer! The fact you might yet be unpublished or are still at University is entirely irrelevant; if you have physically written something within your chosen genre…you are a writer. Think like one!

This is my writer's mindset – I expect to get ideas for chapters and subject matter to include in my books or magazine columns. I focus on writing a lot. Whether I am walking on the beach, waking-up in the morning or having my six-monthly dental check-up…doesn't matter where I am or what I am doing. By expecting to get ideas they constantly happen for me.

If your dream is to be a singer, can you sing? Great, you are a singer! Next take steps to earn your pay from your singing talent. Think like a singer and seek out ways to do what you love every day. Find a manager you can trust if commercial stuff is not your thing. Literally create your dream for yourself. Tell everyone you are a singer and are looking for ways to perform. A way is inevitably about to open for you to sing for the pleasure (and pay) of others.

Doesn't matter what your chosen dream career is, study the mindset of those already within in it.

This is never about losing your individuality, on the contrary you are still going to be the unique personality you always were. Rather it is about gaining the internal programming to adopt the successful mindset, convincing your subconscious to accept the reality of this being exactly what and who you are.

As you are projecting this mindset or Energy - the wider world is also seeing you as exactly the person you desire them to accept you as, reinforcing the reality.

29

TALKING BODY LANGUAGE

Words might well say so much
Body language also speaks volumes.

As a body language expert this seems like the perfect moment for me to show you an almost ridiculously simple way to create a new, improved version of you!

How we stand and present ourselves to the world accurately shows our current mindset. If we are walking around with our hands in pockets, shoulders slumped as we look down at the floor or consistently stand with our arms protectively folded across our body...we are limiting ourselves with our body language.

Yet, what is little known is we can instantly transform our mindset by simply changing our body language!

I not only see if someone of being honest, I can tell what they subconsciously think of themselves and their place in the world.

We have an amazing lever at our disposal here and it really is almost so simple that you might have difficulty in accepting it can make such a radical difference in your life.

It can!

It does!!!

And I urge you to do this even if you a sceptical at first. It is 100% experiential and only once you have put it into practice for yourself are you going to completely get it.

What is this miracle?

Changing your posture CHANGES YOUR MINDSET.

- OPEN GESTURES – when meeting new people or indeed during our daily life, if we constantly fold our arms across ourselves, we come across to others as lacking in confidence, as subconsciously this is how we feel. Same with walking around all the time with our hands stuck in our pockets, this is protective, and others will intuitively pick up on this signal. We can change this body language instantly to transform our internal confidence barometer! I haven't folded my arms for well over twenty years (yes, really!). Any gesture where we cross our arms over our body is making us look and feel insecure. The rather interesting thing about adjusting our body language by not folding our arms and keeping our hands out of pockets, once we get over the strangeness of this new habit, we do genuinely start to feel more confident and empowered.

- POSTURE - How we stand, our posture, affects the way we feel. Observe any of those mega-successful people out there in the big wide world. How do they stand and walk? How is it different from your posture and walk? Chances are, whatever their physical size, they stand up straight and walk tall – meaning their posture is upright, shoulders back and they look the world in the eyes. Again, taking the care to adjust our stance and walk will pay dividends in the terms of the way it makes us feel.

- SEATED POSTURE – my first boss was an expert at lolling in a chair. To the point where sometimes he would actually summersault backwards, and I had to help him up from the floor! In our homes by all means loll away; in the workplace or business meetings we come across as far more empowered if our posture is upright (but not rigid) without arms folded across our body and with our head facing in the general direction of whoever is talking. I know that might seem almost too obvious, that we need to look at the person talking, believe me I have been in front of enough audiences to easily observe who is genuinely engaged within what I am saying and those who are more interested in what they might grab to eat in the intermission. Paying attention means you are mindfully engaged right there in the moment; others will notice and respect your opinion way more.
- SHAKING HANDS – we have all met those bone-crushers who shake hands like they are taking part in some kind of arm wrestling contest. We also know this actually makes them look anything but powerful, instead they come across as a little immature. Then

others who shake hands like a damp dishcloth, while failing to make eye contact. The happy balance here is a firm handshake, eye contact and then let go. We come across as business-like and confident, re-enforcing us being more business-like and confident. How we use body language really does affect our mindset.

- FACE TOUCHING – typical gestures of a liar are nose, mouth or eye scratching, ear rubbing (their own, not yours!) and shifting around within their stood or seated position. There are many more micro-signals, although for our purposes if you witness at least a few of these gestures from someone else chances are they are being economical with the truth. If you find yourself often using these gestures, you might want to look at ways to improve your choice of words to gain more credibility and get your opinions listened to. Consciously avoid face touching gestures or shifting around when talking and you will find yourself quite automatically communicating in an entirely different way.

Taking on board these suggestions will go a long, long way to helping transform your life as you apply them.

Stand-up straighter. Walk tall (whatever your height). Look others in the eyes with a smile. Keep your hands out of your pockets and avoid all arms crossed across body gestures (folded arms/hand clasping in front of you).

This is going to feel weirdly alien at first. Stay with it, you have nothing to lose and plenty to gain…the results we get are the most convincing validation of using body language to change our mindset.

Incredibly quickly your mindset will transform in accordance with your newly adopted positive body language. You feel more confident, in control and others take your opinion way more seriously.

Don't just take my word for it, give it a go for yourself to prove it.

30

NEGATIVE STUFF IS OFTEN POSITIVE

Moving life forward with a lightness of touch
Feeling deepest bliss, note to me "thank you so much!"

No matter how positive our outlook might usually be, it is a fact of life you or I are going to face the occasional challenging event, day or even week. Happens to all of us at some point!

Our mindset can so easily drop back into self-defeating patterns or old comfort traps. Clearly what is needed is a means to get us straight back on track and away from the ever-lurking old neural pathways. We are creating new mind-sets and neural pathways though…

Look below the surface or laterally and there is frequently something positive to be gained from the apparently negative situation stalling our progress for

us. It only takes a little self-training for us to see this truth.

Like with Pete who we met earlier, having found himself made unexpectedly redundant from a job he was great at, he used it as an opportunity to re-assess his life and goals. Pete The Photographer might never have come about had this apparently negative event of redundancy happened.

HITTING THE WALL

Progress can happen remarkably quickly once we are on the right track. We are putting out all that great energy, staying focussed and giant leaps are made towards our dream shortly becoming material fact.

And then frustratingly it all seems to slow down. The momentum we gained stops, maybe even a few steps backwards apparently take us a little further away from where we were so sure we were heading.

Hitting the wall happens to us all. Certainly has with me and look at any successful person in whatever field of activity, they will all have also hit the wall many times and indeed for anyone choosing to live outside of comfort traps it will continue to happen. Go ahead and read a few autobiographies of mega-successful people in whatever field of activity, be it sport, politics or business, and you will be able to confirm for yourself the road to success is seldom straight.

Life is sometimes challenging. However else are we supposed to learn and grow? Hitting the wall is totally the same.

If every conceivable avenue we can think of has been exhausted. And there seems to be no way forward…we have simply not looked at all the possibilities!

Every situation that comes along, especially once we are becoming more consciously aware and evolving within our dream has a solution. Life becomes rather like a multi-dimensional jigsaw and if something in the game of life isn't working exactly the way we wish, then we have obviously put a wrong piece in there somewhere.

Before even attempting to move on take the following exercise:

1. Exam all the actions you have taken so far, get down into the smallest detail, forensically take apart what you did to create the potential stumbling block before you.

2. Is there anything you might have done differently?

3. Is the resultant blockage showing you a possible entirely different direction you can take?

Once you have solved the why of how you apparently stalled (and there is ALWAYS a reason!) and fixed it, then progress continues until the next time lessons need to be learned. Next time around though you will be more prepared and realise the wall is there to force you to create something infinitely better.

Find your way over, around or even under that wall!

When one door closes, we can either open it for ourselves again (it's how doors work!) or go find another which seems more attractive and walk right ahead through that one instead.

KEEP ON KEEPING ON

Truthfully, is there any other realistic option if you or I want to avoid self-limitation?

Finding ourselves in the middle of a metaphorical minefield, then the only possible choice is to carry on and sooner or later the exit is going to be right there! Always is!!!

Deeply challenging situations are there to test our mettle. Although it is natural to falter and stumble, absolutely keep on keeping on. At some point you are going to see that light at the end of the tunnel...it is there every single time.

Furthermore, once we have experienced the very lowest ebb and although life may have been way from easy, having actually survived through the worst and in the end if we have been true to our vision and behaved with integrity no matter what – we will have gained much!

Next time if a comparable situation occurs, its power over us is dramatically reduced. All we need do is remember our past experiences. Know to keep on keeping on and the end is going to be there at some point and more than likely sooner rather than later.

We need a method to help us stay the course...

31

HOW TO DEAL WITH THOUGHTS LEADING TO NOUGHT

Never was anyone else to blame
Personal responsibility to reclaim

Occasionally we all find ourselves in those moments when we feel a little sorry for ourselves or perhaps think that the world is not always quite so fair. Happens to all of us, certainly has done to me and I am sure it's the same for you as well.

Having the odd moments of Thoughts Leading to Nought are part and parcel of our existence as humans. The difference is in our ability to be accepting of these moments. Oh, we can be...**but definitely not for too very long!**

Just as negative thinking can become habit forming, equally so can thinking in terms of positive outcomes and good things coming into our life.

So, next time you are having Thoughts Leading to Nought don't dwell on them or feel disappointed with yourself. Accept this has happened and that is okay because it is all part of being human.

Then instead begin to focus on a positive happening you recently experienced or remember to feel a little gratitude for the good things in your life. Turn away from the bad feelings and you will soon train yourself to have a new attitude. With the right mindset, anything that is possible is possible!

LETTING GO OF VICTIM MENTALITY

The journey of evolving into the ultimate version of ourselves, the person you or I all have the latent potential to be, for sure brightly illuminates any self-limiting mindsets we might be clinging on to in all too startling naked clarity.

Taking one step further into self-defeating mindsets than the temporary Thoughts Leading to Nought is to become aware there exists there within us a more deeply rooted

Victim Mentality. Awareness is a wonderful thing and holds a mirror up to ourselves, showing those areas within us that we need to work on.

A Victim Mentality is the expectation of terrible things happening in life and unfortunately feeling kind of vindicated when they manifest. Victim Mentality is a comfort trap just like any other. One firmly held mindset which serves to keep us equally firmly rooted in self-limitation.

The dweller within Victim Mentality constantly acts out and says negative words, bizarrely quite often seldom even realising they are really behaving in such a self-defeating way. These individuals are genuinely unaware they are doing this as the pattern is so acutely embedded within their thoughts and vocabulary.

Carrie is someone I met who was otherwise positively-minded. Sadly, she had one hang-over from her past in that she constantly used self-defeating language. She asked for help as her life was failing to live up to her expectations and she wondered why. Listening to Carrie talking over the course of a few hours, as she explained the entire reality of her life, I noticed her consistently projecting her negative self-beliefs through her words. Suggesting a new mindset might work for her, Carrie quite forcefully insisted she had already adopted one, this is why she had consulted me as it didn't seem to be working!

And yet paradoxically she completely failed to recognise she ever used self-limiting language when describing herself and her life. I asked permission to record our conversation from that point forward and later playing it back to Carrie finally opened her eyes to the stark reality of how she talked herself into failure.

Once we are aware we are trapped in victim mentality (no more capital letters) we can happily be free to create a new reality. It is going to require willpower to break the habit and constant vigilance. Wonderful if we have someone in our life we can trust to assist in the quest, requesting of them to gently point out any happenings where self-defeating talk enters our vocabulary. Slowly but surely, it is possible to re-programme our thinking and leave victim mentality behind.

The more positive events starting to show forth as our new life experience, even quite early on in the transformational process, lending some greatly appreciated motivation to moving further away into personal freedom.

32

RE-VISITING MISTAKES, RE-LABELLING MISTAKES

Needing to forgive ourselves for mistakes we made
Mistakes are only discovering how to not behave.

Anybody who has succeeded in getting somewhere in life will have a considerable number of "mistakes" behind them.

The big difference between the group mind of the majority of people and these walking success stories is in how they react to mistakes. These people never dwell on their mistakes; they certainly don't see them as failing in any way or spend wasted hours crying over them. Rather they pick themselves up, dust themselves down and move on. Another set of feedback now handily stored away in their subconscious minds, ready to be used next time the occasion arises.

Think about this for a moment. Mistakes can only happen when we are actually taking some type of action. Passively lazing watching tv all day, doing nothing much of anything, certainly never led to anyone to make one of those larger than life mistakes.

So, mistakes can only happen when we are in some way putting energy into our life, making decisions.

For right or wrong, it does not ultimately matter, the fact is to have firstly made that mistake, we had to be already actively participating in our life.

MISTAKES ARE NOT REALLY MISTAKES AT ALL!

Mistakes are signposts.

Mistakes are valuable feedback from any poor life choices, showing us the correct direction to take and the accurate decisions for us to make the next time around.

Poor life choices 99 out of 100 times will be those ones where we procrastinated to intellectually work out the logical direction we ought to take, rather than follow our intuition. How often at some level did we feel unsure or even insecure about the poor choice, but went right on head to do it anyway, because logically it made more sense?

As I have already said mistakes are learning, on one level they are indeed and yet so much more than that besides. Every mistake we make is eliminating another possible pitfall, freeing us up to do more things differently when a similar scenario happens along and make it a success instead.

If you and I wear mistakes on our sleeves we are judging ourselves. Limiting ourselves. Thoughts leading to nought. Got to move on, let them go and appreciate the wisdoms gained. Be grateful because here is now another priceless way to avoid making similar errors in future.

It is how we choose to feel about these moments that determines our future path. Embracing our mistakes and owning them reminds us exactly how to NOT do something. And these are often the greatest gems of information we can get, teaching us far more about ourselves than all the success stories in the world can ever do. We certainly all need to treasure them, never dwell on them and be grateful for the truths they show us!

CLEARING UP

If our mistake (feedback, remember) created a mess we have got to clean up after ourselves before being able to fully move on. This might literally be the lesson needed to be learned by the supposed mistake! Take responsibility for the situation, for our own life and resolve it head on.

Communicating to build trust again is vital. People will usually forgive mistakes, but never being kept in the dark.

Take direct action and communicate your intentions to those who need to know, everyone respects the person who is visibly taking steps to resolve an issue and clean up after themselves.

It is all part of what we talked about earlier – feedback. The whole event is another opportunity for you to shine under duress and brilliantly show the world that this temporary goofing-up moment isn't going to define you. You are a person of integrity who stands tall, takes responsibility for your actions and moves on!

33

THE MINDSET FOR AFFIRMATIONS

Listen to our words and what they say
Creating our reality every single day!

Affirmations are those carefully chosen words or phrases we can utilize to bring about necessary transformation in our lives. Saying them out loud is the usual way to use affirmations.

Much has been written and spoken over the last century or so about the subject of affirmations. Amazing early pioneers such as Florence Scovel Shinn with her Game Of Life books and the later writers who followed her, introduced many to the concept of affirmations as a direct way of positively changing their life.

Affirmations we can either chant or say on a daily basis, however, a word of caution here. **It is the emotions we**

feel that are behind an affirmation which really determines its success, our mindset.

If you or I say an affirmation proclaiming - "I welcome the success into my life!" while holding in our mind a picture of bills which need to be paid, debts or an unhappy relationship, then here we have a mixed message and no amount of chanting about success is going to really change a great deal in our life…

It is the emotions that we feel behind any affirmation which determines the success or indeed, not!

So, if we are going to use affirmations we need to be sure they are ones we can buy-into. Those we believe can genuinely happen for us, because we have to clearly hold a picture of whatever it is we are aiming for in our mind and make it seem as real as we possibly can, all the while we are saying our affirmation.

The way the affirmation might manifest for us is completely unimportant, the vital part is knowing it will happen to the point of **already giving thanks in the words we use for the object of our words being there in our life.** Like "I love driving my classic MG and give thanks for it being parked in my garage" or something else pertinent to your own dreams and desires.

Meditation can help here. When I first started with affirmations a few decades ago, I did find the best time to say them was directly after a meditation. I would have a few cards with chosen affirmations written on them placed by the side of me, so when I had finished my meditation I would then be in the correct mindset to contemplate some affirmations.

If you find, for the moment at least, you can't get into the right mindset for affirmations (and they need to be completely relaxed and never from desperation) then best avoid using them. You really won't be doing yourself any favours and on the contrary, they can actually be more limiting to yourself, rather than achieving anything worthwhile.

Mindset and feeling are all that really matters and the words we then choose to use, to reinforce that feeling.

If you are going to use affirmations, you vitally need to feel the emotions first. Before a word comes out of your mouth, build up the emotion inside of you. Build it up and build it up and build it up. This REALLY matters to me! I need this in my life, this reality in my life!!!

And only then say the affirmation…

You don't need to chant it three thousand times. Once a day is plenty with all this powerful emotion, the feeling behind those words of yours!

The words we choose to use when describing ourselves and our lives matter…a lot! As we will see in the next chapter.

As there has already been plenty written on this subject by so many others, I am not going to suggest specific affirmations here or exact words or phrases, because I trust you will know what is relevant in your life and what will work best for you. Now you will have to excuse me while I go make a classic MG happen in my life!

A QUICK REMINDER ABOUT DECISIONS

You or I need **to avoid at all costs making any important life decisions if we are in emotional turmoil.** Wait a while until things are more stable and relaxed. Then we can attune more with our intuition to make the right choice.

34

WORDS, SO MANY WORDS

Words
Words
Words
So many words
Words of threat
Words of bullying
Words of thoughtlessness
Words can crush any potential

Words
Words
Words
So many words
Words of encouragement
Words of support
Words to lend a loving hand
Words can move any mountain

Be careful what you say for you never know who might be listening...

Others you engage in conversations only hear a small portion, an absolute fraction of your entire catalogue of words spoken each day. You hear them all, every single one.

You are the most important secret eavesdropper on all your private conversations, even those you have with yourself.

THE REAL POWER

Every time we use words to describe ourselves or our lives we are using an affirmation...let's ensure they are good ones!

What we focus on with great intensity, what we give our attention to most of the time **makes us who we are, creating or manifesting the life we live.** Thoughts are only partly responsible, as I know you are beginning to realise. Words are the actual catalyst we use that outwardly expresses our feelings and are effectively the gears that put those feelings into action in our lives.

WORDS CHANGE EVERYTHING

By changing the choice of words we habitually use when describing our life or emotional state, we possess a magical tool to transform that same life.

I AM – two of the most powerful words in existence, for those two words are always followed by a direct reference to how we feel, our emotional response to a situation or our actual wellbeing.

Whatever is added to those two words I AM quite literally ensures directly exactly the experiences we have in life and our success (or not).

So many times, our words are disproportionately over-reactions to the events happening around us.

For sure challenges come along in life, it happens, how we choose to describe those challenges goes a long way to us either feeling worse or finding some inner strength to see the light at the end of the tunnel.

If we describe one of those challenging individuals we all encounter from time to time as "completely messing with my head" or "they make me feel sick!" or worse still "I'm so annoyed I could throttle him". Can you see why these phrases might make the situation feel ten times worse for you?

We use I AM to create our life when we say:

I am sad. I am happy.

I am ill. I am well.

I am bored. I am fascinated

I am poor. I am successful

I am old. I am young

I am shy. I am bold

I am weak. I am strong

I am small. I am worthy

I am furious. I am slightly annoyed

I am unable to cope. I am sure I will cope

I am utterly devastated. I am a little perturbed

I am deeply upset. I am a bit disgruntled

I am completely overwhelmed. I am making an action plan

I am seriously unwell. I am seeking ways to heal

I am totally lost. I am looking for a way

I am full of problems. I am dealing with challenges.

Every time we make one of those big statements, we may well sound dramatic and passionate, but all we are doing is adding way more energy to whatever the issue might be and ensuring we feel considerably worse than we really need to. If we do need to temporarily be around one of those people whose personal energy clashes with our own, how about instead describing the encounter as "slightly challenging" or "a bit irritating" or better still "I am easily able to deal with guys like that, my happiness is down to me!".

How about health issues? If we have a "crushingly dire headache" or a "horrendously debilitating flu" perhaps "devastating insomnia, I can barely keep my eyes open" do you think you or I will quickly heal if this is how we describe how we feel? On the contrary it is going to make anyone feel all the more unwell. How about "slight discomfort in my head" a "cold" perhaps "I will take a quick power nap, then I am sure to feel better".

This subject is so important I have evolved our very own Alternative Word Thesaurus, use it and see what difference this makes in your life. **Give it a go, you have absolutely nothing to lose and might well gain a lot!**

ALTERNATIVE WORD THESAURUS

TRY - trying implies making a half-hearted effort to do something. "I gave it a go, at least I tried". To try can hardly be considered making a determined commitment to succeed whatever obstacles may cross our path, in fact quite the opposite. Try as a word is ultimately rather trying. Some alternative words rather than try or trying are DO, COMMIT, ENDEAVOUR, NOW I WILL, and I NEED TO DO IT.

SHOULD and COULD - is showing a lack of real commitment. "I should wash those dishes" is not going to get those dishes washed. Should implies that for sure in theory we need to do something, but we are not really going to. Could is a cop-out phrase. I could go to University and get qualifications is making a statement about a possibility, without any kind of commitment. Some alternative words rather than should and could are I AM GOING TO, NOW I WILL and MY NEXT TASK IS.

PROBLEMS – ouch! This is going to make anything we need to deal with seem big and scary. "oh, I have so many problems!". We all have things that come along in life we have not anticipated from time to time, it happens. A new way of thinking is needed if everything we encounter is viewed in terms of unsurmountable problems. Far better we re-label it A CHALLENGE. A challenge brings out the best in us, ensuring we go on dealing with it right to the very end. A challenge is motivational, something to solve and see through.

ALARM CLOCK - before we carry on talking about words I will share an example of how a small shift in a label made for a radical shift in my own attitude. Every morning for quite a few years my clock went "brng, brng" and I saw it as an alarm. Now, for me an alarm is something calamitous "Oh no, an alarm!" So, it set me out of bed already alarmed and wondering what next alarming thing was going happen. Eventually I realised this is silly and I re labelled it my WAKE-UP CALL. Every morning it is still the clock going "brng, bring" at that part of the day when I get up, but labelling it a wake-up call, rather than alarm, well that's motivational "what can I do today?". It is inspirational, I have had my wake-up call "let me go and see what I can do to change the World today!" So, just one difference in the way we label something, and for sure, substantial changes can happen in life.

IMPOSSIBLE - if the great thinkers of the past few centuries had subscribed to things being impossible we would not have electricity, xylophones, digital watches, telescopes or any of the billion and one other things we usually take for granted. To the closed minds of those times these great inventions or contributions to the arts must have seemed highly impossible. And yet they happened. Brunel, Einstein or Picasso (and all the other geniuses) must have met their fair share of dream stealers. Thankfully for the sake of everyone else they ignored them. If anything is literally possible in any sense at all, then it ceases to be impossible. It just takes a little determination and surely it can manifest. I am not going to suggest alternative words for this one only a beautifully open mind and reminder of the fact as a rather famous film actress and great humanitarian once said - nothing is impossible, even the word itself contains I'm Possible!

I HATE – oh boy, this one does make me cringe inside and sometimes I cannot help but literally wince to hear people start a statement with those two words, I hate. Do I need to tell you why this is a poor choice of words? It is fine to dislike something or even a person! I hate is such a strong statement to make, so many awful things in the past have been done on the back of those two words, I hate. And it does send out immensely powerful messages about our way of judging situations and people. Plus, by the solid quantum law of magnetic attraction, what energy is put out there by us attracts like energy. If we use I hate as a statement, we are attracting many more things to also hate into our lives. Would any of us really wish to bring more things to hate into our direct experience of life? I sure know I wouldn't! NOT TO MY TASTE is a rather more positive statement. "She is not to my taste as a person" or "that food is not to my taste". Of course, if there is someone or something causing us to genuinely feel such a radically strong reaction as hate we need to remove them or it from our life as quickly as we possibly can!

I DON'T WANT - followed by a statement of intent such as "...to be late" or "...to have to retake that exam" or " to get spots" might be anything. The point here is the sentence that starts with those three words. What we focus on with great intensity becomes our reality. If all your attention is given over to arriving late, failing exams or indeed getting spots that is the Energy you are sending out, and confirming it perfectly with your words. Guess what is going to happen next? You will be late for your exams and fail, because you had to stop on the way to pick up medication for your spots and there was a queue! More positive statements to make here would be "I need to be sure I am on time" "With all my studying I stand a great chance of getting a great grade in my exams" (assuming you did actually study!) and "I am grateful that my skin is clearing and now I want it to stay this way". I'm leaving this one here as I am sure you get the concept now.

IT'S NOT MY FAULT! – making excuses for personally failing in tasks or blaming others rather than taking responsibility for our actions will inevitably bring along continually similar situations until we change that mindset to leave the negativity of passing the buck behind and be free. Lesson learned. If you failed that exam, you didn't study hard enough. If you didn't get that deal at work, you didn't seem like you were passionate enough for it. If you failed to get that hot date with the person you fancied your approach was wrong or maybe they just don't fancy you, in which case it is time to move on. Far better instead I ACCEPT RESPONSIBILITY.

EXPLETIVES - these send out an ugly, jagged energy and as always, come back to the originator as their life experience. Maintaining our cool detachment is occasionally tested to the absolute limit, particularly with certain kinds of people. Walking away can seem fine in theory, yet not always the way the situation plays out for real. What to do now then? Shout and swear? Lose control and rage? Looked at from the larger point of view of quantum reality and energy balancing, that person who caused such a strong reaction from us would have quite rightly crossed our path. How else? If we are to grow as spiritual beings, we are sure going to be tested until we finally get the point. Alternatives to expletives? OH BOTHER! OH MY! or even BLIMEY JEEPERS! If nothing else adopting any of these will take the sting out any situation and more than likely make both parties laugh or at the very least smile.

I FEEL SO ILL - is one sure way of ensuring that we are certainly going to feel worse and take longer to recover. Rather I ALWAYS QUICKLY HEAL.

I'M UNLUCKY - works as a self-fulfilling prophecy, the same as I ALWAYS PUT WEIGHT ON. Russell is a friend who is to all outward appearances the luckiest man ever born. He not only won on the national lottery big time, he then went and did it again within a year! Every time Russell puts a coin into a slot machine he seems to win something. He is also able to eat like he has hollow legs and never puts on a gram in weight. He constantly tells people he is lucky with money and can eat what he wants, never having to worry about getting fat. A fantastic example of Energy in direct action. Russell is completely sincere when he makes those statements, in absolute belief he creates his own reality. Naturally his body and his Energy wave give him precisely what he believes is true. Like Russell habitually says I AM ALWAYS LUCKY, and I AM ALWAYS MY IDEAL WEIGHT REGARDLESS OF WHAT I EAT.

I AM POOR - we may find ourselves temporarily low on funds from time to time, many of us have been there at some point in our life and it rarely lasts for long. Poor is a state of mind and if you think of yourself in such a way I urge you to re-read this book several times and change that mindset forever. Rather I LIVE A RICH LIFESTYLE and ensure it is, which frequently has so very little to do with hard cash and is way more about attitude.

I AM BORED – quite frankly engage with something to improve your life every single day! To be blunt, in my world idle x lazy = bored. Buy-into I LOVE IMPROVING MY LIFE.

SELF PITY – is incredibly self-limiting. Feeling sorry for ourselves is self-perpetuating, until we break the pattern. Far better to go ahead and interrupt our limiting mindset by feeling a little gratitude for the things in life we so often take for granted. Like a roof over our heads, food to eat, friends and family, pets or any of the other thousand and one things we all tend to perhaps take a little bit for granted, yet ought to feel heartfelt gratitude for. I AM FEELING GOOD (sounds a little like the beginning of a cool song) or LIFE IS OUTRAGEOUSLY AWESOME!

PUTTING OTHERS DOWN - if we cannot think of a nice think to say, then say nothing - as the old saying goes. Putting others down always says far more about us than the victim of our words. Would we really wish to be known as insecure and cynical? That is how those who put others down come across, every single time. And untrustworthy as well, naturally some of those things said about us occur behind our backs, would we impart anything of importance to someone who gossips or says negative things to us about mutual friends?

PUTTING YOURSELF DOWN – vitally important for the effect it has on our direct experience of life. This takes the form of calling ourselves stupid or something similar. There is no stupid by the way, if we don't know something it is purely because we have yet to learn it. Does not make us stupid, simply gives us an opportunity to discover something new! Expressing opinions on how awful we look on a day to day basis – these invite everyone else to be critical of us as well. Never, ever label yourself stupid or an idiot! If you want to know more about a subject go and find out, then you are informed. If it fails to interest you, leave it alone and all is good, so what? We don't need to know everything about everything. Plus, if you are always putting yourself down you are personally giving the world and its' siblings the right to treat you badly. Instead I AM EMPOWERED.

RETHINKING OUR WORDS THAT ARE HEARD

The brilliant point you or I need to remember about words is **here is a way that anyone at all can improve their quality of life in ever such a simple way**. Jettison any words or phrases which limit us in any sense, replacing them instead with a more positive use of language.

Free will – the choice is ours. Always!

In addition to the few examples I have given you I am sure when you start to focus your attention on how you express yourself for sure you are going to come up with other words you use which might be limiting you. Those which your gut instinct tells you it is time for you to lose now. Listen, pay heed and simply transform the energy you surround yourself with.

35

DAILY STRESS FREE LIVING

What is false and what is real?
Can we really trust the way we feel?

Part of our experience of living in this third dimensional human form on this bluey-green planet of ours is that we can occasionally find ourselves feeling a little or perhaps even a lot stressed. If this is just going to be a short-term situation more often than not it is something we can deal with, let go and leave behind. Frequently with the simplest of changes in our routine or approach we can not only reduce the ability of stress to affect us, but also rather happily free ourselves from the stress of getting stressed in the first place!

Continual stress has been medically proven to negatively affect our wellbeing by causing mental health issues and

293

our body by breaking down our immune system, often leading to serious illness if left unchecked. There are some clear warning signs we need to take heed of, which are signals from ourselves that we are perhaps experiencing more stress than is healthy.

These include:

- Excessive anger, we can all lose our temper from time to time and this is perfectly normal, but if we are continually raging at all around us, then there is something behind that.
- A sense of frustration, a kind of giving up with life "oh, I can't do anything, it's just like that!". It is never just like that and for sure things can change. This attitude is usually a sign of stress.
- Insomnia, we all have the occasional sleepless night, but if we are continually experiencing difficulty in sleeping then something has to change, because that is definitely unnatural. So, if you are suffering from insomnia there will be a reason behind it.
- Lack of concentration or difficulty in taking in any new information. Presented with the instruction manual for a new electronic device, if the words all sort of jumble together and we are

having difficulty taking the information in, this can also be a sign of stress.

- Poor eating. Not feeling hungry or indeed over-eating can both lead to their own issues in the long term. If we are experiencing issues relating to eating, just not feeling like food or difficulty in digesting what we eat, leading to stomach ache or under/over active bowels, there might well be stress behind it.

- Headaches. Stress and tension cause headaches. And as someone who did used to suffer from tension related headaches I can certainly empathize with anyone going through the same challenging experience!

Just some of the more obvious signs that stress can be affecting us.

THE QUICK TWO-MINUTE DE-STRESS

Before we move on, I want to give you something which, although never intended as a long-term cure, represents a more instant way of just taking yourself away from a stressful situation, calming things down for yourself.

This is a method I have developed and refined over three decades, it is called The Quick Two-Minute De-Stress.

So, you or I find ourselves in a temporary situation where our anxiety and stress levels have risen beyond what is normal and healthy. Perhaps it is just one of those days, one challenge after another has presented itself and we feel like we are about to go pop!

The Quick Two-Minute De-Stress

Sit still and close your eyes.

Concentrate on the colours you can see behind your eyelids, even if this is only black, no rules here. Whatever colours you see is fine.

In your mind start to count slowly back from 30 to 0.

30 (pause and breathe) 29 (pause and breathe) 28 (pause and breathe) 27 etc. until you eventually reach 0.

When you have arrived down at 0, you can open your eyes.

Many people, from all walks of life have found this simple little exercise incredibly useful. **It is something I**

have been teaching for a good few years and everybody who has given it a go has found some benefit from it.

The beauty is it can be practiced almost anywhere at any time. I mean clearly when it is safe to do so – if you are driving please find somewhere safe to park-up first or if operating heavy machinery, please move away before starting The Quick Two-Minute De-Stress!

On a more serious note though, feel free to share this once you have proved to yourself it works. The more people who know about The Quick Two-Minute De-Stress the sooner we can collectively bring a little more peace into this World...

DEALING WITH STRESS

So, now we know the potential negative effects stress can have regarding our wellbeing, what can we personally do to reduce stress in our everyday life?

Stress is not something it is possible to avoid, however, there are definite methods we can use to reduce the stress when relating to how we approach situations and challenges. These can take the form of handling our emotions, ways of dealing with things in a more controlled way that works for us rather than the situation controlling us. And there are also some conveniently practical methods we can use to bring down our stress levels.

Over the next few pages are some suggestions and coping methods for handling stress, they are presented in no particular order of importance or priority. Take on board the ones relevant to your life and use them.

EVERYBODY GOOFS-UP SOMETIMES

We have all done it. Made those decisions that if we could only go back and change things, we might have done things differently, said something different or maybe not even said anything at all!

You and I need to ensure these goofing-up moments never define who we are now. Yes, for sure, on that one occasion we did not necessarily do things with the best of intentions, perhaps for ourselves or even others. Or else we just downright made a mistake!

As we learned earlier mistakes are only learning how to not do things.

Even life coaches goof-up! Failing to back-up the files for my this very book led to me losing nearly a year's worth of manuscript after my computer crashed to the point of oblivion. Starting from scratch again ended up my only choice. I sure learned that lesson!

We have all experienced goofing-up…mistakes or failures never, ever define who we are. EVER! But they can make us wiser.

RELATIONSHIPS

If our relationship is the cause of stress, honesty with how we are feeling and frankly communicating this is so freeing. If this can be done without resentment or hostility.

We need to be honest with ourselves about what we truly feel and once we are true to our inner self, share this calmly. If our relationship is the cause of stress, then in all likelihood our partner is going through a similar reality.

Sitting down and talking is the beginning to resolution. However, and whatever within these discussions ultimately plays out obviously mutually matters a lot, but at least the fact you are now sitting and talking means that something new is going to happen.

Resentment can build up through lack of communication and if everyone knows where they are at least resolution can happen. You can both transparently see where the relationship is going to go.

It can potentially bring you closer, as you understand one another a little better now, or if the relationship is genuinely not fixable then you can both let go to be happy elsewhere.

SETTING ACHIEVABLE TARGETS

Setting realistic goals is incredibly motivating and de-stressing.

Write down all the things that you need to do within a day. I have been doing this for a good few decades. Every single night before I even contemplate sleep or going to bed, I jot down a list of all the actions I need to take the following day. When I get up in the morning I then know exactly what I have got to do.

If every task we must perform is written down in a list, they can be ticked-off one by one as they are achieved, that is incredibly motivating. I can speak from personal experience here. And this is a majorly de-stressing thing to do, write lists, because we know exactly those tasks we need to perform each day.

SLEEP

Sleep is essential if we are to function to the best of our ability. Sleeping when tired if at all possible. Sleep is regenerating.

There are some methods we can use which will help us have a good night's sleep. When suffering from insomnia, and we have probably all been there at some point, I know I have…it can seem unending!

A crucial step is to avoid coffee or any caffeine rich drinks for at least four to five hours before retiring for bed. Drink something else instead, chamomile tea is excellent, very relaxing. Have a chamomile tea an hour or so before you are contemplating retiring for the night.

Take a warm shower. Leave aside any invigorating shower gels, instead something more relaxing to put you in a chilled mood. A nice warm shower, with calming shower gel will put you more in the mindset for sleep.

Essential oils can help as well. Never put them directly on your skin. Place a few drops of lavender essential oil (if you like the aroma) on a handkerchief or tissue, place this under your pillow where you are still able to smell it, but it is not overpowering, helps the mind get into a more relaxed ready-for-sleep state.

I have found one of the methods which works well for me is to meditate myself to sleep. Which is to start at a thousand and gradually slowly count backwards to zero. I do generally find long before I have even reached back to nine hundred I am fast asleep!

MEDITATION

Those who meditate are usually more relaxed. More of which in the next chapter!

EXERCISE – GETTING OUT WHAT WE PUT IN

Exercise is vitally important for maintaining a healthy body and strengthening the immune system's ability to stay strong.

If you are feeling stressed, go and take at least a half hour walk.

There are other ways we can exercise. Swimming is absolutely brilliant. If you can swim, go swimming two or three times a week – great exercise and with so little stress on the body while we are doing it.

Other forms of exercise include dance – if dance is your thing check-out local groups you might like to join or simply dance around your house. It will still be benefitting you and make you feel good!

Tai chi or yoga practised in their higher form are a type of meditation, as is aikido. Golf – not only excellent exercise, but a mind work-out as well.

MIND WORK-OUTS

Sudoku, crosswords or all other kinds of intellectual puzzles will keep the mind active and help with brain-training, lending us the potential to deal with any potentially challenging events in a more ordered way.

OUTSIDE STIMULANTS

Relying on drink, drugs or smoking to cope with stress are never going to benefit any of us in any way at all and will just add issues which will need to be addressed at some point.

HOLISTIC THERAPIES

There are a whole range of therapies which can help us relax more to deal with stress.

An aromatherapy massage is wonderfully soothing. Most towns and cities have an aromatherapy clinic, find one with all the official certifications hanging on the wall and book a session. You will surely feel better for the experience and it costs very little proportional to the relaxation achieved.

Deep tissue massage and reflexology are infinitely calming.

AND FINALLY

If you are finding it difficult to deal with stress, and are feeling continually overwhelmed, nothing seems to help – do go and take yourself off to your chosen healthcare professional who will be able to refer you on to a professional stress consultant or other therapist they feel is appropriate.

36

MEDITATION BEGINS RIGHT HERE

Whatever journey he undertakes
Wherever he goes, he meditates.

I am going to share with you my own personal method of meditating…

This has evolved with me over the course of more than thirty years and naturally still continues to develop, providing new forms of enlightenment along the way. All of those I have taught this method to have been able to meditate almost straight away and subsequently adapt what they have learned to suit their own needs.

In meditation there is no right or wrong, it is the level of understanding and personal experience or insight that ultimately matters the most. In explaining my own methodology, I merely show one possible path. There are many others, if my method doesn't speak to you then I strongly recommend exploring further until you find one that does fit you perfectly.

Experience has taught me that the road to evolvement is experiential, requiring dedication and commitment.

Sacrifices will have to be made. Yet like in all good things in life, those sacrifices are generally willingly made in order for the greater understanding that ultimately results as the end manifestation.

A personal example would be in terms of a lot of popular culture and by this, I mean most television programmes and a fairly large proportion of commercial radio-friendly music, which jars quite significantly with my desire to reach the ultimate level within my well-being and evolve into the best version of myself possible.

Negativity of others no longer affects me in the way it once did; other than to feel a deep sense of compassion, sending love and, as a body language psychologist, I am at least able to see where their behaviour and reactions more than likely originate from.

MEDITATION BEGINS RIGHT HERE

In my talks, my classes, I have had people say to me "Dean, I would love to do meditation, to practice meditation, but I have tried it and it doesn't work for me, my mind is still too busy, and I can't relax".

There are no rules when it comes to meditation, other than what we personally get out of it. This is not an intellectual exercise, like I once did so many of us do attempt to intellectualize it into oblivion, meditation is experiential. It isn't something where we sit and think "now I am going to meditate, and I will get this, that or the other from it", We really do have to go with the flow.

This might end up being one of the shorter sections of this book, because meditation is remarkably simple when broken down into its component parts. The real enlightening moments, of course, come later as we gain more experience, to become more adept at reaching an ever deeper meditative state.

So there really are no rules, in fact, if you can breathe…you can meditate!

It really is as simple as that. The other thing I would say before we get into the practicalities is that I am not a practicing Zen Buddhist. I am happy to admit though I do get much of the Zen life philosophy - especially their concept of mindfully enjoying the journey to our destinations in life, seems like a good attitude to adopt to me. I am still not a Buddhist all the same.

I have taught meditation to people from all walks of life and religious backgrounds.

Meditation doesn't have to be a religious thing, for sure it can be part of a religious practice, but it doesn't need to be. It can be easily integrated into most belief patterns as simply taking some down time, to clear our minds and move forward afterwards with less stress. As a stress relief I would say that meditation is absolutely vital!

NOW LET'S MEDITATE

You can sit cross-legged on the floor, as you have doubtless seen in photos, via the internet or television, that classic meditation posture or just sit in an upright chair. Hold your hands on your lap, with your fingertips and thumbs touching. Initially focus your eyes on an area of the ground about a metre in front of you, as you begin to concentrate on only your breathing.

Without thinking too deeply about it, give your entire attention over to purely the function of breathing. Breathe deeply and slowly. Calming your thoughts as you start to relax. At some point you might like to naturally close your eyes. And continue focussing purely on your breathing. If any day to day thoughts attempt to intrude, re-apply your attention to breathing, count your breaths, one…two…three and so on. When you count your breaths, after a while the outer reality of life will start to retreat, and you will find that you are actually deeply meditating! You can continue for as long as feels comfortable and to end simply open your eyes.

Meditation is never a time to mull over material thoughts or for finding the answers to challenges in our lives, what it is though is a means of heightening intuition or if you prefer, our gut feeling – which must be of far more use to us in the long run. Indeed, the answers you or I seek when we are no longer stressing about them, will invariably come via our intuition and again, invariably these are going to be the right choices for us to make.

As I mentioned, some treat meditation as an intellectual exercise, this will never work. Nothing could be further from the truth. Meditation is hands-on and is down to our own experience of us practising it.

I have been meditating since my late teens, which is a little while ago. And if I do miss meditation for some reason or another, I do feel a significant difference, it helps me to keep a perspective on life really and I meditate every day whenever I am possibly able to do so. It need only take fifteen to twenty minutes out of our daily schedule, for the benefits we gain, I can confirm it is definitely worth it.

37

BUTTERFLY MINDS

*Nobody said everyone's dream needs to be the same
find yours and that is what you aim to live!*

So, there we all are putting out that fantastic energy and yet things seem to develop so far…then…slowly…stop.

Some people seem to have this immense difficulty in deciding what they really want from life and change their minds every other week about:

A. What kind of career they would like.
B. Where they wish to live and in what kind of house.
C. What success means to them.
D. Which car to drive.
E. If they wish to be single or married.
F. What kind of further education to enrol for.

G. Or even what kind of parties the will host once they are a millionaire!

You get the picture, keep changing our mind and all our personal energy is dissipated.

To go through building our focussed energy up all over again as we home-in instead on the latest version of the new successful life we wish to live…until the next time you or I change our minds…and then it all needs to start over once more!

Spend seriously fun time mapping out what you genuinely want your life to be. Rather than metaphorically deciding you want a beach house and a week later realising a penthouse apartment is quite cool, so you will have that instead…and then the next week perhaps after all you will just live on your yacht-with-a-view…do your best to stick to your dreams.

That is why it is vitally important, before even beginning on the path to personal freedom, to at least have some vision of where you are actually heading!

<u>Those routes to getting there evolve as we travel towards dreams</u>, which is a different matter altogether and as we have already seen throughout Alive to Thrive this is truly an essential part of the process.

In the meantime, it's extremely useful to keep at the forefront of your mind when thinking about the future you are shaping for yourself **this or something even better!**

Then if the personal concept of your own success is any way inadvertently limiting all that you might TRULY achieve – you are instead allowing your even potentially higher achievements the opportunity to really happen!

CONTROLLED POWER

If you lose control of yourself, you lose control of the situation and your ability to be empowered. Anger and frustration take away your personal power...always.

SPIRITUALLY SUCCESSFUL

We have all have more than likely met a few of those single-minded spiritually focussed people. They all share one thing in common. They devote themselves solely to personal development with the utmost zeal and are like sponges soaking up ways to grow. The other personality trait they unfortunately share (and express this often) is how they certainly do not need money and in fact dislike having possessions. You guessed it, they are all struggling financially to get by.

Often some people seem to be under the illusion that spirituality and success are somehow separate entities. Maybe we can have one or the other, but definitely not both. This is patently untrue, for absolute proof of this make the time to read a few autobiographies of those hugely successful ethical business people, martial arts legends and global adventurers. You all know the ones, those individuals who became materially successful without every sacrificing the core essence of their ethics, who they are within themselves or how they choose to treat others.

It has even been suggested money might be in some say the root of all evil. Wow! Talk about setting up a self-defeating negative vision of success! I would have thought rather that possessive greed and failing to use wealth to help others is surely way more negative-minded.

Money has energy which is neither positive nor negative of itself. It is what WE choose to do that determines the frequency of our wealth energy wave and frankly more importantly if our success makes us feel happy and healthy.

Money doesn't care if we are devoutly religious, on our own personal path to spiritual enlightenment or at the other end of the scale eschew spirituality all together.

We all have the freedom of choice to grow into our dreams and if that includes being wealthy then we all begin from the same starting place, regardless of background. It is all about mindset and listening to our intuition to guide us into direct action when required. Changing the energy of our lives always requires we first act to transform things anew.

The sponge analogy I used before is good, let's adopt that. How about becoming sponges to soak up anything which can help us grow as individuals? Whatever that personally means to you or me.

If that might be financially, spiritually and ideally both simultaneously!

38

MORE OF WHAT MAKES YOU FEEL GOOD, LESS OF WHAT MAKES YOU FEEL BAD

Follow your bliss so they say
many a truth spoken in cliché.

Seems obvious really, doesn't it? Spending more time doing the fun stuff and less time involved in anything which makes us feel bad. And yet is this simply an avoidance technique? A burying our head in the sand kind of false utopia?

Well. No, not really.

Remember earlier on when we talked about the Zen way of looking at life and enjoying the journey? Now is the time for us to finally put that philosophy to good use to allow us a beautifully proportional view of our own life.

HOW WE CHOSE TO LOOK AT LIFE

In Zen philosophy every front will have a back.

In other words, for all those thrilling moments of high achievement, those which make us feel amazingly energized and wonderful throughout every atom – there will also have been all that background work enabling us to get there.

Or finding we are finally capable of running a marathon, to cross the finish-line with a personal best time, will have surely required months of preparation reaching that level of fitness.

And in all honesty what would be the point in finding all the backroom work, those less glamorous yet necessary tasks, utterly dull and boring?

Do you imagine you or I will be in any way functioning to the best of our ability if we are only giving half our attention to those vital building blocks for our own success and cannot wait to get on with the more glamourous stuff?

On the contrary, whenever we find ourselves involved in the more day to day routine, yet which in however small a way adds to our bigger picture, **we do ourselves a great favour by fully engaging with the process and better still by finding something to enjoy within it.**

DO WHAT YOU ENJOY

It is all about that living in the moment and giving our complete attention to the task in hand. This turned out to be one of the trickier lessons I needed to learn. When dealing with essential research for my wholesale business I would be constantly focusing on two hours down the line when it became that part of the day to follow up on phone calls. "Get this out of the way then I can go and do the interesting stuff" was how I tended to look at this task.

This all changed when I had my eyes opened by a colleague to the reality of the truth that all this research was in fact where most of our new business originated from and then further the realisation dawned on me that I actually enjoyed the creative challenge of the research as well!

I can tell you I sure gave it my full undivided attention from that point on and this enabled us to reach brand new territories for business in Ireland, Spain, Sweden and Canada.

FOR THE MOMENT

I make a point each week of washing my own car. Sure, I might easily take it along to the guys near where we live who do a great job. I prefer the manual task of taking my car from dirty to gleaming myself. I find some manual work integrated into my weekly routine helps tremendously to keep my feet nicely on the ground. And by focussing my entire attention on the job in hand for an hour or so I do genuinely feel the exercise is so much more than ever only taking exercise. Personally, it keeps me in touch with my fourteen year old self with his first business washing cars for half his neighbourhood, reminding me to stay awake to opportunities.

What manual task can you invest yourself completely in? Giving your entire attention to what you are doing and choosing to enjoy the entire process from start to end? Find something and give it a go, I promise you it will help you apply that same level of involvement in all areas of your life.

THEN AGAIN

There are some tasks which no matter how well our attitude of gratitude might work, regardless of undertaking them with a fixed smile upon our face or even doing our best to see the bright side of – we simply plain dislike doing!

Avoid those things which continuously make you feel down or unhappy.

How? Well, can the task be delegated? Or simply left undone?

Kevin had two tasks in life he got no pleasure from and they had genuinely begun to make him feel depressed as he didn't see how he might avoid them. A successful builder, he had acquired a beautiful house with an equally beautiful expansive lawned garden and Kevin disliked mowing grass with a passion. As an inherently practical hands-on kind of guy, it had literally never crossed his mind to employ a landscape gardener to take care of it all for him. Now with one thing which made him feel bad out of the way, next we needed to address his biggest dislike of all, the one which sometimes kept him awake at night. Which would be dealing with the financial book-keeping for his business. Starting out as a sole trader, as his business had grown to employing over twenty tradespeople, so had Kevin's headache about keeping his accounts records up to date. Again, his mindset had yet to catch up to his success! Suggesting to Kevin his time would be better served supervising his team and getting out giving quotes for gaining potential new clients; and this would be so much easier for him if he employed the part-time services of an accounts clerk to take care of the admin for the business. Two overwhelming burdens from his life removed by leaving those tasks he loathed to other people who actually enjoy them! Win/win.

www.deanfrasercentral.com came into being out of my dislike for administrational tasks and a happy by-product is it has made me massively more efficient with my time.

Focus on what you enjoy doing and if at all possible delegate or pass across those tasks you personally find unremittingly dull and yawn-inducingly boring to someone who instead enjoys them.

YOU NEVER LOSE

My grandmother's favourite saying was **what is for you won't go past you** and how true this is.

An old friend, Neil finally got his degree in graphic design and applied for a position within the Advertisement Agency where he had already completed his work experience and figured it was a forgone conclusion his new career awaited him. To only be told they were unable to offer him a job for the foreseeable future as they had all the designers they needed. Although initially somewhat taken aback as this metaphorical door slammed in his face, Neil eventually picked himself up and started to look around for the first time at what other opportunities might be out there waiting for him. After a few interviews, none of which ignited much spark of interest in him, along came the opportunity he was compelled to say yes to, fitting him perfectly. Joining the small team of three designers within an international freight company – their role essentially to design all the internal and external documents/brochures for the business. This also meant he needed to travel extensively across much of Europe and the Middle East on a regular basis. As Neil loved to travel, having actually spent his gap year back-packing across Europe, his new career proved to be fulfilling in a multitude of ways!

If you get turned down for the university of your choice, you were never there in the first place, therefore you have lost nothing. You are still in precisely the same position as before you applied. Nothing changed. Go ahead and keep on applying to other universities, eventually one of them will be exactly the right one for you.

Similarly, if the woman/man of your dreams turns down the offer of a date, you were not going out with them before asking. And you are still not going out with them and so nothing really changed.

FOOD FOR THE SOUL

What do you love to do? Where do you love to go? Do you have a favourite way to spend your down-time?

Do more of all those things!

You deserve to spend your life doing anything which makes you feel awesomely good!

THE FINAL WORD ABOUT TOXIC PEOPLE

Make the conscious decision to spend as little time as you are able in the company of toxic people and feel how it is like a weight being lifted from your shoulders.

How about if this toxic person is a close family member, like a parent or some other close relation? Minimize their effect on you by realizing they clearly have issues, none of the negative energy they project is truthfully anything about you – and still avoid spending too much time with them if you possibly can!

39

DETACH FROM HOW

Living within the energy of conscious creation seeing the signs as they are shown, which they surely will be.

Time to bring together all we have covered in our journey through Alive to Thrive relating to leaving how things happen on the way to our goals more open-ended, to then allow all the fun stuff to happen!

For sure this can be something of a fine balancing act and at first seems to make practically no sense.

Our goals and dreams ought to be all consuming, for sure, knowing here is something that truly deeply matters, the manifesting of which is passionately important.

Fine, all is good and as it needs to be.

THE ART IS IN DETACHING FROM THE HOW IT IS LITERALLY GOING TO PLAY OUT IN REALITY

We need to give our beautifully projected energy the chance to work and standing over the outcome, impatiently waiting to see the results, is showing a lack of belief in all the good stuff coming our way.

Absolutely being prepared to take direct action when it is clearly the right time is the way to go. In the meantime, let the ingredients we have blended together work and turn our attention away for now.

There is always something else you or I can do to prepare for the steps we will soon need to take. Like getting fitter or developing an ability to meditate allowing us to tune-into our intuition easier.

The way it will manifest down the line is the job of the energy wave we have put out there into the universe - our role is to be ready.

Remember also to expect your vision of the ideal future or for something better! That way if your path is to experience unimaginably brilliant manifestations of your dreams, then you remain open to receive them.

Detaching never means to stop caring – rather having put out that great energy, to step aside slightly and now allow it to happen.

> This method takes practice…the end game is worth the effort…you put out the energy and step aside…wait for that clearly defined moment for action…and it will arrive…always does!

40

SLOGGING AWAY IS NEVER THE WAY

Passing the point of intuition, to reach the point of initiating what will be and being open to the consequences of those decisions.

There is common misconception that if we wish to achieve a measure of what it typically means to be materially successful this is going to necessitate us slogging away and working practically 24/7.

Quite simply this is untrue.

For sure it is useful to help manifest our goals by having a strongly developed work ethic, yet at the other end of the scale there is never the need to suffer for dreams and let career matters lead to sacrificing our daily quality of life.

> **In fact, following our dreams needs to ADD to our quality of life, rather than making it worse.**

As one who once worked 15 hour days and took my work with me wherever I went (even on vacation!) I can entirely appreciate it might seem like we need to invest all our energy in our goals.

And yet…

Thankfully those days are far behind me. I write most days, I promote my work most days either giving interviews or networking; and if I instead feel like going for a walk or travelling somewhere interesting – that is exactly what I do (www.deanfrasercentral.com having made sure I first see to any definite commitments!).

> **Love what you do it will never feel like life is one hard slog. And never feel burdened by your dreams – if you ever do feel that way it's time to find new dreams.**

PLAY TO YOUR STRENGTHS

If you have been reading this book in order and started to put these principles into practice in your own life, you will have confirmed this for yourself by now - **the key to being happier, healthier and above all more successful is to play to our own strengths.**

To remind you of what we covered earlier, entrepreneurs seldom make the best hands-on managers – oh for sure they can be amazing motivators of other people, getting them to buy into their ideas. Being stuck piloting a desk every day of the week and being obliged to sign off on every single minutest working within their business would more than likely make them scream.

The same with any career endeavour or indeed, walk of life. By far the most useful wisdom we can gain is what are our core strengths and then mine them.

There will also be some things we either have zero interest in doing or, as we are being honest with one another, we are pretty darned awful at!

Take another look at your things outside of your skill-set list you made earlier. To remind yourself one more time of those things which don't work for you. Make sure your life is built around stuff which you enjoy and grow your success through utilizing your own unique individual talents. This together with the self-discipline to stay on track ensures life will change, for the better…

I find pointless small talk, remembering minute details (it's why I always keep a notebook), micro-managing and being willing to say no if offered an opportunity to talk at an event or in the media - all outside of my own skill set. Fortunately, I have people around me to fill the gaps with their own skills and often stop me when my enthusiasm sometimes gets the better of me when offered a chance to say YES, if I already have other commitments and explain to me I actually cannot be in two places at the same time!

Now you can discard forever the things-outside-of-your-skill-set list! Keep your mind focused on what you can do and find others to fill the gaps within your own skill set when required.

As we have established ALL the great sports men and women make a vocation of playing to their strengths. As do all of the genuinely successful in any kind of career…and that goes a long, long way to guaranteeing they love what they do!

41

CELEBRATE YOUR SUCCESSES AND BE READY FOR MORE!

You did it! Now let's party!!!

LIFE IS STILL ABOUT THE JOURNEY

Please do remember to remember this. Although the ultimate destination is wonderful, also take the time to vitally enjoy the process of living each day to get there.

> **Each time you achieve some notable success...a further step towards your end game...it's time to CELEBRATE!**

This can be any type of significant milestone - like passing exams, getting a step-up in your career, earning that first 100k or even becoming fit enough to run the New York marathon.

Whenever a life achievement is gained it is time to acknowledge it and find some outrageous way to mark the occasion. One that you and everyone else will remember for a long time:

- Can be taking your family or friends for a fantastic night out at an exclusive top class restaurant.
- Going with your significant other for a deeply relaxing pampering weekend experience at a five-star spa or wellbeing centre.
- Or if the event is truly exceptional, booking a out of this world vacation at such an amazing destination you and your closest will be thrilled just at the prospect of spending time there, with a departure date as soon as possible.

Celebrating needs to essentially be some event you might never have even considered prior to your new-found success. Whether that's a private box at the theatre to see a Shakespeare play in Stratford-upon-Avon or a weekend shopping experience on 5th Avenue in New York, it crucially needs to be something which reinforces on so many levels how your life is different now and this event validates the proof of it!

If pays to make our own successes events everyone can enjoy, and the great energy created by family and friends joining with us to celebrate our achievements will only add to the self-fulfilling effect of yet more success waiting for us…and crucially open their eyes to their own long-held dreams becoming possible.

Win/win all round then!

42

IT NEVER FINISHES, THOUGHT I HAD BETTER LET YOU IN ON THIS SECRET!

Creating their lives and circumstances
Thoughts and words acting like magnets

When you have finally seen those long-held dreams realised, and by following the steps throughout Alive to Thrive you certainly stand a good chance of them finally coming to be your life, then other dreams you might never have even imagined becoming possible, gradually organically proceed to take pride of place as future goals.

It really does never end and indeed quite right too, it truly never needs to!

High achievers in life will constantly set themselves new challenges or targets to achieve and keep their motivation going all the way to their completion.

Once you have personally witnessed a few of those once seemingly impossible dreams come to pass in your own life, you find yourself happily in a position to stretch your expectations even further within whatever outrageously awesome new goals you're able to achieve!

And then set out once again for the next chapter of this great adventure called your life.

AND FINALLY, TRULY LIVE YOUR LIFE

Whatever your birth certificate might have the world believe...always stay enthusiastic to remain young inside.

Look back when you are ninety and feel although you've achieved great things...you have many more left to do!

TRANSFORM YOUR MINDSET - CHANGE YOUR LIFE FOREVER

About the Author

I love to inspire others.

I realize how fortunate I am - I love to inspire others. My creativity through writing and my live events (presentations or poetry) enables me to show others possibilities for how their lives can be dramatically improved.

I strongly believe in our own inner guidance, at some level you and I do know what is really right for us.

The choices we make, creates the life we lead. Why not make that life as magical and wonderful as possible?

Sound good?

I show possibilities and decisions we can all choose to take...life is essentially all about our choices.

The only constant in life is change, and I adore this paradox! If something in our life doesn't work for us we can choose to change it...either literally or through adopting a more empowering mindset.

Peace and Love,

Dean Fraser

www.deanfrasercentral.com

Although the author and publisher have made every effort to ensure that the information in this book was correct at press time, the author and publisher do not assume and hereby disclaim any liability to any party for any loss, damage, or disruption caused by errors or omissions, whether such errors or omissions result from negligence, accident, or any other cause. This book is not intended as a substitute for the medical advice of medical professionals. The reader should regularly consult a chosen medical professional in matters relating to his/her health and particularly with respect to any symptoms that may require diagnosis or medical attention.